GOLFER'S GUIDE
SPAIN

GOLFER'S GUIDE
SPAIN

MORE THAN 100 COURSES
AND FACILITIES

DAVID J. WHYTE

NEW
HOLLAND

First published in the United Kingdom in 2002 by New Holland Publishers (UK) Ltd
London • Cape Town • Sydney • Auckland

Garfield House	80 McKenzie Street	14 Aquatic Drive	218 Lake Road
86–88 Edgware Road	Cape Town 8001	Frenchs Forest	NSW 2086
London W2 2EA	South Africa	Australia	Northcote, Auckland
UK			New Zealand

www.newhollandpublishers.com

1 3 5 7 9 10 8 6 4 2

ISBN 1 85974 277 7

Edited and designed by Design Revolution, Queens Park Villa, 30 West Drive,
Brighton, BN2 2GE on behalf of New Holland Publishers (UK) Ltd
Publishing Manager: Jo Hemmings
Series Editor: Kate Michell
Project Editor: Nicola Hodgson
Editorial Assistant: Anne Konopelski
Designer: Paul Bowler
Design concept: Alan Marshall
Cartographer: Patrick Vigors at Map Creation
Picture researcher: Penni Bickle
Production controller: Joan Woodroffe

Reproduction by Pica Digital Pte Ltd, Singapore
Printed and bound in Singapore by Kyodo Printing Co (Singapore) Pte Ltd

Photographic Acknowledgements
All photographs taken by David J. Whyte except:
Front Cover Allsport; pp.13, 14, 20, 28, 46, 88, 89 Spanish Tourist Board; pp.25, 118 top
James Davies Worldwide Photographic Travel Library; pp.30, 45 Catalan Tourist Board;
p.40 Real Club de Cerdanya; pp.68, 118 bottom Eye Ubiquitous; p.92 Empics Ltd; p.102
Vista Hermosa Golf Club; pp.113, 115 The Scottish Golf Photo Library; p.123 De Lugo
Golf Club; p.125 La Toja Golf Club; pp.147, 148, 149 Tenerife Golf; p.151 Salobre Golf
Club; p.153 Craig Robertson

Front cover: Valderrama, Sotogrande; Spine: Amarilla, Tenerife; Back cover: (top) La Manga, Murcia, (bottom left)
Alicante, Valencia, (bottom centre left) Catalonia, (bottom centre right) Costa Adeje, Tenerife, (bottom right)
La Guardia, Pontevedra, Galicia; Title page: Alhaurin Golf, Andalucia

Contents

HOW TO USE THIS BOOK

Finding Your Course

The courses in this book provide a selection of the best golf available to visitors. They are grouped into seven chapters to help you plan an itinerary. The courses in each chapter are presented in, as near as possible, a geographically continuous order.

Major courses such as Valderrama or El Saler have been given more in-depth descriptions along with a diagram of the course layout. The selection of other courses reflects the author's opinion of those that should be played. However, there are nearly 300 golf courses in Spain and many others are worth visiting.

Key to Distances

Spanish courses are measured in metres. Very occasionally they also post the distance in yards. As a rough guide, add 10 per cent to the metre distance to give an approximate yardage. The indicated length of each course given in this guide is the maximum length either from the white (medal) tees or from the championship (tiger) tees. As in most countries, visitors are normally required to play from the forward visitors' tee.

Club Facilities

Most Spanish golf clubs offer a range of facilities and it is only the more remote or smaller clubs that do not cater for golfers' usual requirements. Changing rooms are commonly provided with showers available.

Catering at Spanish clubs is normally of a high standard with even the smallest clubs offering a bar and patio restaurant to relax in after a round. Generally restaurants attached to better clubs are a worthwhile alternative for evening dining.

Most clubs now offer buggies. Pull carts are also usually available for hire. Most shops attached to golf clubs are well stocked with immediate necessities as well as a good range of clubs and clothing.

Visitor Restrictions

Spain's courses are divided into two main groups. Most, especially in the busy tourist areas, are aimed at the tourist market, while others, especially around major cities, cater for members only. Some members' clubs allow access to visitors if they show a handicap certificate and there are tee times available. Other clubs are exclusively for members and their guests.

At tourist-oriented courses competitions are often held. It is wise to telephone in advance to arrange your golf – the earlier you book the better. One thing to bear in mind is that there is a growing pressure on tee times in certain popular areas. If you are a competent group of golfers, try to get early tee times as you may find the pace of play significantly slower later in the day. Some clubs consciously try to put low handicappers out early. If you are booking your own golf it is advisable to let the course know your handicaps and that you would be keen to play as early as possible.

As with most golf clubs, a reasonable dress code is expected. You may find Spanish golfers slightly more relaxed in attire, but jeans, trainers, collarless shirts and sandals, despite the warm weather, are not acceptable. Soft spikes are now universally accepted here and the pro-shop or starter will insist that your metal spikes are removed and replaced with more environmentally sound soft spikes. This can take a few minutes and you might miss your tee time so have your spikes changed before you go on holiday.

Handicap certificates are rarely requested at tourist-oriented courses but every serious golfer should travel with theirs to avoid disappointment.

Key to Green Fees

£ = £10+
££ = £20+
£££ = £30+
££££ = £40+
£££££ = £50+
££££££ = £60+
£££££££ = £70+
££££££££ = £80+
£££££££££ = £90+
££££££££££ = £100+

The green fees indicated above refer to a weekday round at typical times. Besides these price structures many courses offer Twilight Golf or versions of this with much reduced fees for golf and carts especially during the less busy summer months. Credit cards are not universally accepted, so check when booking.

Foreword

Exploring the geography of Spain golf course by golf course is one of the most gratifying experiences there is. North to south, east to west, the range of golfing opportunities our country has to offer is sufficient to satisfy the most demanding of tastes. Difficult courses, enchanting courses, courses that hold within them myriad secrets – which this superb book reveals through its beautiful pages.

The reader will be guided at his leisure round these extraordinary places, places that every golfer will relish before allowing himself to be seduced – golfing bag safely back in the car or the hotel – by all the other compelling facets of our country.

Just one suggestion, though I'm sure it goes without saying: don't forget to pay us a visit.

Emma Villacieros
Presidente, Real Federación Española de Golf

Introduction

Golf in Spain

Occupying the southwest corner of Europe, Spain is the continent's third largest country after Russia and France. It is comprised of 17 Autonomous Regions (Comunidades Autónomas), the island groups of the Canaries and the Balearics and the city enclaves of Ceuta and Melilla on the North African coast. All these regions possess a rich diversity of culture, climate and landscape.

Spain as a whole has a fascinating history. Set at the gateway to the Mediterranean Sea and separated from North Africa by only 14km (9 miles) of water, it has been a crossroads in the history of civilizations, particularly because of its close relationship with the Americas and with the rest of Europe.

Once considered a 'poor relation' within Europe, Spain has changed considerably since the years of General Franco's dictatorship, and is now a dynamic, prosperous and stylish country.

More than 45 million tourists visit Spain each year, and many of these visitors come for golf. Most golf tourism development has been in the Costa del Sol (often dubbed the Costa del Golf). Other developing tourist areas on the Iberian peninsula also often use golf as their main attraction, and the construction of golf courses is usually included in their initial phases. Coupled with the attractiveness of Spain as a warm and welcoming holiday and residential destination, Spain remains a pleasant and popular country in which to enjoy a game of golf.

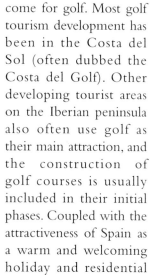

It is now not only tourists who want to take part in golf. Spaniards' enthusiasm for the game has also grown, fuelled in part by the success of local heroes such as Seve Ballesteros, José María Olazábal and Sergio Garcia. Golf has become a boom sport, and on local courses young hopefuls hone their skills with ball and club.

Left: Golf del Sur on Tenerife offers crisp greens and fairways emphasized by black volcanic bunkers. Above: Mijas Village is a busy but charming diversion.

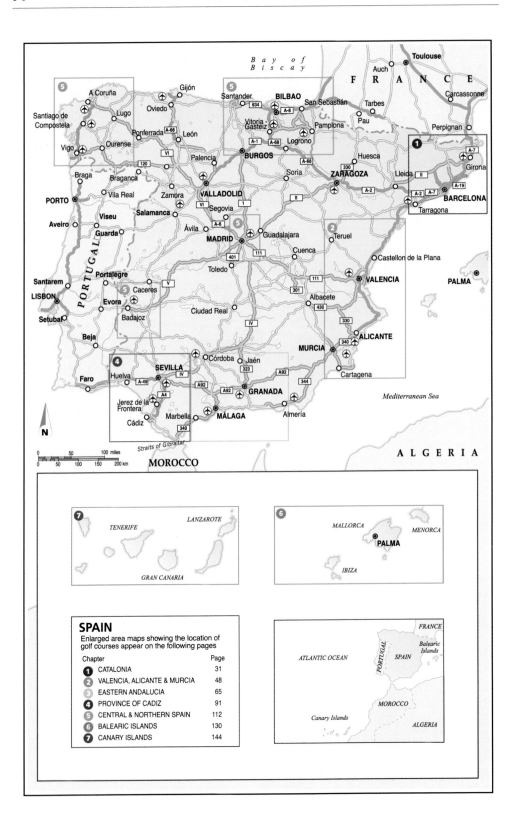

Bay of Biscay

TOULOUSE
Auch
F R A N C E
Carcassonne
Perpignan

Santander BILBAO San Sebastián Tarbes
Pau
Pamplona

A Coruña Gijón
Santiago de Compostela Lugo Oviedo
Ponferrada León
Vigo Ourense

Vitoria-Gasteiz Logroño
BURGOS
Palencia

Huesca
Soria
ZARAGOZA Lleida Girona
BARCELONA
Tarragona

Braga Braganca
PORTO
Vila Real Zamora VALLADOLID
Segovia

PORTUGAL
Aveiro
Viseu Salamanca
Guarda Ávila MADRID Guadalajara Teruel
Cuenca Castellon de la Plana

Santarem Portalegre Caceres
LISBON Evora Toledo
Setubal Badajoz Ciudad Real
Beja

Córdoba Jaén
SEVILLA
Faro Huelva
Jerez de la Frontera
Cádiz Marbella MÁLAGA Almería
GRANADA

Albacete
VALENCIA
PALMA
ALICANTE
MURCIA Cartagena

Mediterranean Sea

N

0   50   100 miles
0 50 100 150 200 km

Straits of Gibraltar
MOROCCO A L G E R I A

⑦ TENERIFE LANZAROTE
GRAN CANARIA

⑥ MALLORCA MENORCA
PALMA
IBIZA

SPAIN

Enlarged area maps showing the location of golf courses appear on the following pages

FRANCE
ATLANTIC OCEAN PORTUGAL SPAIN Balearic Islands
MOROCCO
Canary Islands ALGERIA

GENERAL TRAVEL INFORMATION

Most golf visitors fly into one of Spain's major airports and either rent a car or, if taking part in a package holiday, take a coach to their accommodation. Independent travellers will also find a well-coordinated transport system.

The main international air hubs are Madrid and Barcelona. Most cities and popular tourist destinations also have their own airports and are well served by scheduled and charter services. Spain's road and rail networks have greatly improved over the past decade. Rail and coach services are efficient, and mainland Spain has good ferry connections with the UK, North Africa and the Balearic and Canary Islands.

TRAVELLING TO SPAIN

By Air

Almost 30 per cent of international travellers to Spain arrive by air. More than 50 million passengers land or take off from Spanish airports, with nearly 70 per cent travelling on non-scheduled charter flights.

Scheduled Flights

Most international carriers offer services to Spain or connect with one of their partner airlines. The Spanish national airline, Iberia, offers daily scheduled flights into Madrid and Barcelona from all Western European capitals. British Airways offers scheduled flights several times a day to Madrid and Barcelona from either London Heathrow or London Gatwick. British Airways' franchise partner, GB Airways, offers more than 50 weekly flights from London to southern Spain. From the USA and other parts of the world, most international

AIRLINE TELEPHONE NUMBERS FROM THE UK
Iberia: 020 7830 0011
www.iberia.com
British Airways: 0845 7733377
www.britishairways.com
GB Airways: 0845 7733377
www.britishairways.com
Go Airlines: 0845 6054321
www.go-fly.com
Easy Jet: 0870 6000000
www.easyjet.com

carriers offer a partner service with connections from the main European cities. American Airlines connects with British Airways in London, allowing 'seamless' transfers through London and on to your Spanish destination. Iberia offers direct flights from the USA into Madrid and Barcelona.

Budget Airlines

Budget airlines from the UK such as Go or Easy Jet offer economic, no-frills flights to many destinations in Spain. Some operate on a seasonal basis. For the short flying time involved and considering the cost savings, they represent excellent service and value. Go Airlines offers return flights from London to Bilbao from £70. They also cover Barcelona, Madrid, Málaga, Palma and Alicante. Go Airlines seems to offer the best service with the most up-to-date planes.

Charter Flights

For access to the coastal resorts of Spain, regular charter flights serve the regional airports of Reus (for Tarragona and the Costa Dorada), Girona (Costa

Brava), Alicante (Costa Blanca), Almería (Costa del Almería), and Málaga (Costa del Sol), as well as the Balearic and Canary Islands.

Ferries

From the UK, Brittany Ferries offers twice-weekly crossings between Plymouth and Santander in Cantabria. P&O European Ferries sails from Portsmouth to Santurce, near Bilbao in the Basque Country. These crossings take more than 24 hours. The ships offer cabin accommodation as well as a swimming pool, gymnasium, restaurants, cafes, shops and a cinema. These services are busy in the summer months, so it is best to book well in advance.

Brittany Ferries: 0990 360360
P&O European Ferries: 0990 980980

Trains

If travelling by train from the UK it is necessary to travel via Paris and then on through Hendaye in the Pyrenees to San Sebastian or via Cerbère and Port Bou to Barcelona. Trains from London, Brussels, Amsterdam, Geneva, Zurich and Milan all reach Barcelona via Cerbère. At Cerbère there are connections with the TALGO and long-distance services to Valencia, Málaga, Seville and Madrid, and other major destinations. Sleeper services on the TALGO from Paris allow you to travel without having to change trains.

International Rail Enquiries: 0900 848848
Channel Tunnel Rail Enquiries: 0990 186186

Travelling by Car

If you wish to bring your own vehicle to Spain, the options are to take the ferry services arriving on the north coast or drive via the French motorway system. You can drive via Bordeaux then on to San Sebastian and Madrid then south. Alternatively, for the south coast, head for Perpignan in southeast France and continue on to Barcelona, Alicante and south on the *autopista* to Málaga. Both routes require two or three days from London, allowing for breaks and overnight stops. A green card is required from a motor insurance company in order to extend your comprehensive insurance cover for such a journey. Most major insurers operate a rescue and recovery service within Europe but this must be arranged before travelling.

TRAVELLING WITHIN SPAIN

By Aeroplane

Domestic air traffic tends to concentrate on Madrid-Barajas Airport, which handles 2.5 million passengers per year. The busiest routes, apart from the Madrid-Barcelona shuttle, are the Madrid-Balearic and Madrid-Canary Island runs. Frequent shuttle services are offered via the main domestic flight operators such as Iberia, Air Europa, Air Nostrum, Aviaco and Spanair. These are fast and efficient with tickets either booked in advance or paid for at the terminal. Two Iberia-affiliated companies operate connections to the Balearic and Canary islands: Binter and an air charter company, Viva.

Airport telephone numbers

Alicante: 966 91 90 00
Barcelona: 934 78 50 00
Bilbao: 944 86 93 00
Madrid: 913 05 83 43
Málaga: 952 04 88 38
Palma (Mallorca): 971 78 90 00

Above: Hórreos such as Hórreo de Iglesia, Pontevedra and Vilanova de Arousa are ancient granaries.

Las Palmas: 928 57 90 00
Santiago de Compostela: 981 54 75 00
Seville: 954 44 90 23
Tenerife Sur: 922 75 92 00
Valencia: 963 70 95 00

TIME ZONES

On the Spanish mainland and Balearic Islands, local time is one hour ahead of Greenwich Mean Time in winter and two hours ahead in summer. The Canary Islands are on GMT, except during the changeover to summer time when the clocks are put forward one hour, with the result that island time is always one hour behind mainland and Balearic time.

Ferries to the Balearic and Canary Islands

From Barcelona and Valencia there are regular sailings to the three main Balearic Islands. Trasmediterránea ferries operate a car and passenger service that takes around eight hours. The sailing is usually calm. There are also regular services between these islands.

From Cádiz on the southwest corner of Spain, Trasmediterránea (914 23 85 00) operates weekly services to Las Palmas on Gran Canaria and Santa Cruz on Tenerife on the Canary Islands. The crossings take around 39 hours, but the ships are well fitted and offer amenities such as shopping, cinemas and restaurants. The same company runs passenger services between the islands of Gran Canaria, Tenerife and Fuerteventura.

By Train

The Spanish State Railway offers superb, high-speed services within Spain. TALGO and AVE are the main high-speed services between large cities and are fast, reliable and comfortable. The regional and local services, however, tend to be very slow and generally not of use to visitors unless they are travelling short distances between towns.

RENFE Information and Reservations:
Barcelona: 934 90 02 02
Madrid: 913 28 90 20
Seville: 953 74 38 24

Above: The town of Cedeira in Galicia marks the beginning of a series of beautiful duneland beaches and lagoons.

By Car

The advantage to golfers of having a vehicle at your disposal is obvious. Many resort areas have fleets of the smallest vehicles for their general holiday business. If there are two or more of you golfing you will need a mid- to large-size vehicle – a B Group will possibly prove too small for two golfers, clubs and luggage. MPVs and mini-buses can also be arranged for small groups of golfers.

The best car hire deals are usually booked as a fly/drive package through your travel agent. International car hire companies such as Avis and Hertz are found at most airports with offices also in main towns and tourist destinations. The system is efficient and you will be in your arranged vehicle within minutes of checking in at the car hire office. Avis seems to offer the most comprehensive service in Spain with major depots and an excellent collection/drop-off service at each airport.

International Reservation Numbers
Avis: 0990 900500 (in Spain – 900 13 57 90 – toll free)
Hertz: 0990 996699 (in Spain – 900 10 01 11 – toll free)
Budget: 0541 565656
Europcar: 08706 075000 (in Spain – 915 56 15 00)

Atesa Car Hire (in Spain)
Barcelona: 933 02 45 78
Bilbao: 944 42 32 90
Madrid: 915 71 32 94
Seville: 954 41 97 12

Driving in Spain
There are 7000km (4350 miles) of highways (toll motorways, freeways and dual-carriageways) that make up the main road network. This highway system makes it possible for the visitor to drive in comfort from the Pyrenees all the way down to Andalucía, either along the Mediterranean coast or inland via Madrid. The highway system offers comprehensive en-route services.

Bringing Your Own Car
If you bring your own car to Spain you must observe several requirements. Spanish law demands that you carry in your vehicle its registration document, a valid insurance certificate and your driving licence. Another form of ID such as your passport or a national identity card is also essential. You must display a sticker with the car's country of registration on the rear of the vehicle.

Headlights of right-hand-drive vehicles must be adjusted or deflected with black masking strips that can be bought at ferry ports and on ferries. In case of breakdown you are also required to carry a warning triangle, spare light bulbs and a first-aid kit. As in the rest of Europe, it is compulsory to wear seat belts both in front and rear seats.

Driving in Spain can be a slightly different experience from the UK or USA. There is a noticeable machismo present, often based on the size and model of the car you drive and whether you are worthy enough to be overtaking the 'competition'. On the *autopista*, the fast lane is reserved for this type of lunacy and it is best to stay out of its way.

Traffic regulations are similar to those throughout Europe, as are road signs, although there are some idiosyncrasies to observe. If you wish to turn left across the path of oncoming vehicles you may have to turn right into a turning bay and stop until the road is clear in both directions. This allows traffic behind you to flow on.

Speed limits are as follows:
120km/h (75mph) on *autopistas* (toll motorways)
100km/h (62mph) on *autovías* (non-toll motorways)
90km/h (56mph) on *carreteras nacionales* (main roads) and *carreteras comarcales* (secondary roads)
60km/h (37mph) in built-up areas.

Speeding fines are paid on the spot at 1000 pesetas for every kilometre per hour over the limit. Tests for drink driving and fines for drivers over the blood/alcohol legal limit, which is 80mg per millilitre, are now applied.

Taxis

It is feasible to hire taxis from your accommodation to your golfing destination and back again, and for two or three golfers this can work out to be quite cheap. Often taxis in Spain are large vehicles such as Mercedes Benz estates and there is plenty of room for three or four golfers and their kits. Mention when booking if you require a larger vehicle. Taxis are subject to the fare shown on the meter. In some cities there is a luxury-style service, known as 'grandes turismos', that charge higher rates.

ACCOMMODATION

There is a very wide variety of accommodation available in Spain. The tourist boom that took off in the 1960s has continued unabated and cranes can still be seen building new hotels, villas and time-share complexes in and around every popular area. Since the criticism levelled at the Spanish tourist industry in the late 1980s and early 1990s and the consequent fall in tourist numbers, standards of accommodation have improved. Prices range from £40 per night and up, often with half-board. A seven per cent VAT charge is also added.

Hotels

Hotels are graded by the government and awarded one to five stars based on their level of facilities. Spanish hotels are generally good value for money and it is rare to find one that is shabby. They cater to every taste and pocket, from the most modest (one-star) up to the most sophisticated (five-star deluxe).

Golfers tend to migrate to specific areas and hotels in such resorts are geared up to facilitate their needs, such as storage of clubs. Through the winter, many hotels, especially along the Costa del Sol, want to attract golf tourists and provide extra incentives such as transport to local courses and tee-time booking. In some cases they offer reduced green fees at local courses. It is worth contacting these hotels via the Internet or by telephone to compare the price of a 'do-it-yourself' package with tour operators' prices. Keep in mind, though, that tour operators command percentage discounts and they can work out to be cheaper.

Most hotels have a restaurant service on the premises, with the exception of the *hoteles-residencias* (Residential Hotels). These tend to have a cafeteria where breakfast is served. The best hotel deals seem to be on half-board basis where massive buffet meals are served as well as hearty breakfasts. These are fine if you are happy to eat in the same restaurant each night, but golfers tend to enjoy exploring the joys of the local eateries. In Spain you never go far wrong doing this.

Holiday Villas and Apartments

In the areas around golf courses, it is often possible to rent a flat or villa. This kind of accommodation is often an attractive proposition for families or golfing groups. Rates are set according to season, location and in-house services.

Fincas or converted country houses have become very popular on Mallorca, for instance, and these can add a special touch to your holiday.

Paradores

Spain's *Paradores* are a unique state-sponsored series of 85 hotels specifically built or occupying converted castles, mansions or other historic buildings. These *Paradores de Turismo* are scattered across Spain where the visitor has the chance to sample the regional cuisine, architecture and culture. The *Paradores* in Málaga (see p.70–1) and El Saler (see p.52–3) near Valencia have their own golf courses, and the *Paradores* system now offers around 30 golf courses in conjunction with a set group of *Paradores*. As well as offering high standards of accommodation in unique buildings, they can include booked tee times and significant reductions in green fees. For example, staying at *Parador* de El Saler allows a major reduction in fees, bringing it down to below £10 per round.

The Málaga *Parador* was established in conjunction with the town's thriving wine business. With only 60 rooms, it

Above: Marbella's old town offers a pleasant retreat in Plaza de los Naranjos (Orange Square).

supplies top quality service along with tranquillity and one of the nation's best golf courses.

Paradores Reservation Centre:
Tel: 915 16 66 66
Fax: 915 16 66 57

DAY-TO-DAY ESSENTIALS

Spain's currency is the peseta. Coins come in 1, 5, 10, 25, 50, 100, 200 and 500 peseta denominations. Banknotes are issued in 1000, 2000, 5000 and 10,000 peseta denominations. Spanish banks are usually open from 08:30 to 14:00 Monday-Friday. Some banks in popular resort areas open for longer hours and on Saturdays at the height of the tourist season.

When changing money or traveller's cheques take your passport with you. Beware of hefty transaction charges, especially in hotels. Money can also be exchanged at travel agencies and hotels outside banking hours. Look for a 'Cambio' sign. Cashpoints are found everywhere and provide a reasonable rate depending on the exchange prices when your credit card company processes the transaction. Credit cards are widely accepted. Visa and Mastercard are the most established, but Eurocard and American Express are also useful.

Electricity

Spain's electricity supply is 220 volts. A travel converter plug is required to use appliances from abroad. These can usually be purchased at airport outlets before departure.

Visas and Passports

Citizens of all EU countries, Norway and Iceland do not require visas to visit Spain. This is also true for visitors from Canada, the USA and New Zealand if you are planning to visit for fewer than 90 days. Visitors from other countries, including Australia, must obtain a visa before travelling. Longer stays require that you contact the Spanish embassy in your country before you travel – in fact well in advance to obtain the appropriate visa documents.

Embassies and Consulates

Nearly all foreign consulates and embassies are located in Madrid. Some countries also have consular facilities in larger cities such as Barcelona and Seville. There are also consular offices in popular tourist destinations such as Costa del Sol and Palma.

EMBASSIES IN MADRID

The following is a list of embassies in Madrid. In addition, local police stations will be able to tell you the telephone number and location of the nearest embassy or consulate.

Australia: Paseo de la Castellana 143
Tel: 279 85 04
Canada: Nunez de Balboa 34
Tel: 431 43 00
Ireland: Claudio Coello 73
Tel: 576 35 09
South Africa: Claudio Coello 91
Tel: 435 66 88
UK: Fernando el Santo 16
Tel: 319 02 08
UK Consulate: Marques de la Ensenada 16
Tel: 308 52 01
USA: Serrano 75
Tel: 577 40 00

Tax-free Goods and Customs Information

The 'Tax-free For Tourists' sign you will see displayed in various shops applies to non-EU visitors who can reclaim IVA (VAT) on certain purchases. A tax exemption form is obtained on making the purchase. On leaving the country, upon request, a customs officer will stamp your form and payment will be forwarded either by mail or to your credit card account.

You will find many electronic shops in places such as the Canary Islands and on the mainland. If you are thinking of buying any goods, check the prices with your local dealer before you leave – the saving may be minimal and the stock older than currently available in your own country.

Health Care

The E111 form entitles EU residents to free medical treatment within the EU. This guarantees emergency cover, but it is worth ensuring that health cover is included in your travel insurance package. Healthcare in Spain is excellent, but hopefully you will not have reason to use it. Use sunblock and keep well covered on your first few days of playing golf to help you to avoid sunburn. Alcohol on the golf course should be avoided, especially if you are in charge of a buggy. It is essential through the hot months to take water with you out on the course. Very few courses have halfway houses, or drinks buggies that make the rounds.

Hospitals, doctors and pharmacies are all easily accessed.

Police

Spanish police officers can be very helpful. There has been a noticeable change since the 1980s, when police in many tourist destinations were criticised for their attitudes. More police have been employed to deter petty crime and they seem to be better trained in public relations.

Tourist Information

All popular destinations, major towns and cities have tourist information offices. Hotel foyers usually act as distribution points for brochures on local attractions, and hotel clerks are a good source of information regarding restaurants and other amenities. There is a flourishing publishing industry catering for tourists in areas such as the Costa del Sol or Mallorca with plenty of useful golf guides and magazines. There are also English-speaking radio stations that are a good source of information.

Newspapers

In most parades of shops in popular tourist destinations you will find outlets selling foreign newspapers. Newspapers are also available in hotels, but they are usually one or two days out of date. Some international titles such as the *International Herald Tribune*, the *Financial Times* and the *Guardian International* can be found on the day of publication. In some areas you will find English-language newspapers catering for expatriates.

Shopping

There are few bargains to be had while shopping in Spain for clothes or accessories. Prices are about the same as in the UK, although wine, cigarettes and fuel are cheaper. If you are travelling to Gibraltar these commodities, along with spirits, are cheaper, so stock up.

Self-catering apartments, hotels or villas will have small *supermercados* either attached or nearby, but these are very expensive and the assistants in busy resorts are often surly. Find out where the locals' supermarket is. They usually have more choice and much better quality produce than tourist supermarkets. Their prices are much keener too.

Opening Hours

The tradition of siesta still holds strong, particularly in the south of Spain. As the Spanish tend to stay up late they don't function well until around 10:00. Shops tend to open between 09:30 and 13:30, then from 16:30 to 20:00 from Monday-Saturday. In busy tourist areas this is often extended until 22:00. Department stores and other major outlets are generally open 10:00-20:00 Monday-Saturday. Large department stores and supermarkets are open on some Sundays.

Bars and restaurants generally open from noon until late. Restaurants in the popular tourist areas serve lunch between 13:00 and 16:00, but outside these areas it is unusual to take lunch before 14:00 and more likely around 15:00. If you get hungry between meal times, try a tapas bar. There are dozens of these in any town where you can eat a fairly hearty meal for a reasonable price.

Dinner is served early to cater for the tourists, but real Spanish food is best found between 21:00 and 23:00. Locals congregate around 20:00 to talk, drink and usually smoke with no sign of eating until 22:00 or later. Nightlife in Spain is in a class of its own, particularly from Thursday to Sunday. Pubs, late-night *bares de copas* and discotheques normally stay open until 03:00 or 04:00. In major cities, there are numerous nightspots that remain open until dawn. Drunkenness and unruly

Below: Galicia's western coast is pierced by inlets and ports, such as the port of La Guardia, Pontevedra.

behaviour is unusual in most Spanish towns and cities. Unfortunately, this cannot always be said for the tourist districts.

Pharmacies usually open from 09:30 to 13:30 and 17:00 to 20:00, though in the bigger cities several remain open round the clock. There is a rota, displayed outside pharmacies and published in the daily press, indicating which pharmacies are on night service and/or open at the weekend.

Tipping

All catering establishments in Spain include service in their prices. Nevertheless, leaving a tip is the norm in bars, restaurants, hotels and taxis. The amount you leave depends on your generosity, but between and five and 10 per cent is usual.

Telephoning to and from Spain

Apart from booths (*locutorios*), there are standard public telephones, from which calls can be made to any part of the world. You will need 5-, 25-, 50- and 100-peseta coins or phone credit cards, which can be bought at branch post offices (*estafeta de correos*) and tobacconists (*estancos*).

International calls made from a public telephone box to EU countries are relatively cheap. The boxes take the usual coins, but make sure you have plenty of higher denominations for international calls. Phonecards are more convenient and can be bought at news-stands and post offices. Beware of using your hotel phone for foreign calls as the surcharge can be excessive. To phone abroad from Spain, dial 00 (International) and then the country and city codes, and, lastly, the subscriber's number.

THE FIESTAS OF SPAIN

Fiestas are a phenomenon in every part of Spain. If you are relaxing in your hotel and are suddenly startled by what sounds like gunfire, don't worry – it will probably be a fiesta starting up. These take place very frequently. They most often have a religious or historic basis, perhaps featuring the re-enactment of a famous battle or some macho rites of passage with bulls.

If you wish to call Spain from your home country, dial 00 then the country code, 34, followed by the subscriber number. The number for directory information in Spain is 1003, for information on all national and international codes.

Emergency Telephone Numbers
National Police: 091
Fire Brigade: 080

Ambulance services vary from location to location, so consult the local telephone directory.

Golfer's Insurance

While general travel insurance is always recommended, golfers might wish to check that they are also covered for loss or damage to their clubs in transit, in the clubhouse, while left in a car and for third party liability should they be unfortunate enough to inflict damage to another individual or property on or near the golf course. Such policies might also offer some cover of bar expenses following a hole-in-one!

In the UK:
Golf Guard: 0800 581801

GOLFING IN SPAIN

Over the past 30 years, Spain has become one of the most popular golfing destinations in the world, especially for British golfers seeking an alternative to muddy or frosty fairways during the winter months. Now that the golf boom has swept through the rest of Europe and Scandinavia, particularly Germany and Sweden, golfers from these countries are also joining in. Following the Ryder Cup at Valderrama in 1997 there has also been a noticeable increase in American golfers eager to experience the courses, culture and cadence of Spain.

The Spanish Golf Federation has adopted the Royal and Ancient/US Golf Association rules, so your rulebook still applies. A major change for UK and American golfers is the use of metres instead of yards (add 10 per cent to the metre figure to get a close approximation of the yardage – 150 meters equals around 165 yards). Another change for American golfers is the colour of the tee markers. In Spain as in most of Europe, white indicates the professional tee; gold or yellow is the normal visitor's tee, and red is the ladies' tee. The fairway-markers measuring the distance to the green is usually to the front of the green (this can vary from course to course so if you are a stickler for precision check at the pro-shop). The red post marks 150 metres (165 yards) and the yellow marks the 100-metre (110-yard) point.

A word about greenkeeping; it is easy to be critical of the conditions you might find, but for most of the year there is often a water shortage. While greens and fairways are almost always kept well watered, it is not unusual to find areas of rough and carry left to fend for themselves. Standards seem to be improving, however, and sourcing waste-water from nearby hotel complexes would seem to be an environmentally sound solution.

PLANNING YOUR GOLFING HOLIDAY

Best time to Play

Golf on the south coast of Spain has become essentially a winter sport and this is high season. From November and especially in February and March golf courses are busy with visitors from colder northern countries. Costa del Sol and other parts of Andalucía are the most popular golfing areas, but Catalonia, the Balearics and the Canary Islands are catching up as they increase their number of courses.

Through the day during the 'high season' there is no special time to play except that, like many courses, members may have times booked in the morning. As always, book well in advance – before you travel, advisably – to ensure tee times to suit. If you play through the summer months then tee times around 08:00 and 16:30 are the most comfortable. These are also the most popular times and slots might not be available. However, generally summer is surprisingly quiet on most courses and it is rarely difficult to get on. Play in shorts, take plenty of fluids out on the course with you, and, if available, use a buggy where cooling breezes will keep you more comfortable. Sunblock is also necessary.

Apart from the 'Pay & Play' or 'Daily Green Fee' facilities you will find green fees at the weekends are sometimes twice the cost of a weekday green fee. As with most countries, the weekends are the domain of club members; if you can get a tee time, it will be at an inflated cost.

Rental Facilities

Most clubs offer the usual accoutrements of golf to rent such as hand trolleys, electric trolleys, motorised buggies, clubs and occasionally golf shoes. Buggies average around £20 to rent although in summer there are often good package deals where golf and buggy hire for two people comes at one much-reduced price.

Caddies

Caddies can be found at some clubs, predominantly those with a wealthy local membership. Spanish caddies rarely speak English and so it is harder to elicit the nuances of the course from them.

What to Wear

Golfing in Spain is a relatively casual affair but this is no excuse for untidy or unsuitable attire. Shorts are almost essential as the weather gets hotter. Some clubs will not allow collarless shirts (despite recent professional trends) or jeans. Otherwise the rule that prevails is common sense, but in the face of increased pressure on the etiquette of the game, please keep up reasonably high standards. Perhaps if you dress and behave like a professional you will play like one.

Handicap Certificates

It is highly recommended that a handicap certificate be brought on a golf holiday to any part of Spain. The better courses such as Valderrama or Sotogrande will certainly ask to see an approved official document. If you wish to participate in the many open tournaments that are held, you must bring your handicap certificate.

UK GOLF TOUR OPERATORS AND USEFUL WEBSITES

Longshot Golf Holiday
01730 230370
www.longshotgolf.co.uk

Specialist Tours Ltd
01422 846611
www.specialist-uk.co.uk

Barwell Leisure
(La Manga, Almenara, Valderrama, Sotogrande)
020 8786 3083
www.barwell.co.uk

Linksland Golf Travel
01575 574515
www.linksland.com

Premier Iberian
0800 7833097
email: info@premieriberian.co.uk

Bill Goff Golf Tours
0800 6520968
www.billgoff.com

Golf Reservations Europe
0700 0181818
www.golf-reservations.co.uk

Other Useful Web Addresses
www.golfinspain.com
www.golfspain.com
www.golfiberia.com
www.solweb.com
www.iberia.com

Spanish Golf Federation
Captain Haya
9 5 28020 Madrid
Tel: +34 91 555 26 82

PGA European Tour
Av, Josep Tarradellas, 16-18, 4t 1
08029 Barcelona
Tel: +34 93 410 83 56
Fax: +34 93 410 88 45

Eating in Spain

Eating in Spain has as much cultural significance as it does in France or Italy. The Spanish certainly enjoy food and fine dining, and most visitors make wonderful discoveries of the highest levels of gastronomy.

The Spanish expect to eat good food and it is rare to find poor standards. Even in airports or in supermarket restaurants you will find a decent meal at a reasonable price (although the same might not always be said of motorway (*autopista*) service areas). If you are travelling by car, get on the adjaent C-route and you will soon come across a local roadside restaurant that is more appealing.

The best cuisine

In general, to experience the best of Spain's cuisine, look for small, out-of-the-way restaurants and ask local people for recommendations. If you are looking for fine dining, again away from the main tourist haunts, prices will compare well with other Western countries. However, in the southern coastal regions such as the Costa del Sol, it might not be easy to find restaurants frequented by local people, as most of them come in from Málaga to work in the resorts and head home again when their shift is over.

Fish dishes

Fish (or *pescado*) dishes are always available along the coasts but also in cities such as Madrid. *Pescado Romesco* is a popular if sometimes pricey speciality of the Tarragona region of Catalonia. Restaurants pride themselves on how fresh their fish is and will delight in telling you of their relationship with the local fishermen who supply them daily. Fresh fish kept on ice are usually presented to you at the table for inspection and selection and then cooked to your specification. Other typical dishes to sample are gazpacho (a chilled soup) and tortilla, a potato omelette.

TAPAS BARS

Much is made of Spanish tapas bars in tourist brochures and holiday programmes. The tradition of tapas is basically a ruse to keep customers drinking - much like offering salty peanuts or potato chips — only the Spanish do it with much more class.

At one time tapas were served for free but this is rare now. However, these tasty snacks are usually reasonably cheap and even if they are 'bait' to keep you drinking in the bar, they are a pretty good deal.

There is much competition between bars to lure clientele by producing the tastiest tapas. The variety is endless and might include octopus, spicy chorizo (cured meat), goat's cheese and all kinds of seafood.

Some bars boast as many as one hundred different types of tapas.

Occasionally tapas bars are expensive, but this will be immediately obvious by the décor and clientele. It is always worth asking prices beforehand, as they are not usually displayed.

It is possible to spend an entire evening in a tapas bar eating the equivalent of a very hearty meal for around £10–15. The custom of tapas bars also offers sustenance to visitors in the long hours between meals, bearing in mind that breakfast is non-existent, lunch is late and dinner often borders on bedtime.

Above: Spanish cuisine can be a simple affair employing only the freshest of local ingredients.

Paella

Paella is perhaps Spain's most famous dish – to foreigners at least. However, it is not always easy to find good paella. Valencia is the city where the dish originated but even here, in the midst of the tourist development, true paella is a scarce item. However, the area surrounding Valencia is renowned for fresh, wood-fire paellas and not the sticky rice porridge version that you often find. Head for the village of El Palmar near the golf course of El Saler for a great choice of restaurants with many producing the real paella as well as many other local delights.

Fresh paella is usually prepared for a minimum of two people and if you know this is what you want it might be worth warning the restaurant in advance.

Spain's Best 18 Courses

This selection of courses is based on playability as well as general factors such as friendliness of the club, scenic beauty and accessibility to golf visitors. You will notice, therefore, the omission of some major venues such as Valderrama which is expensive, difficult to get onto and difficult to play (for both professionals and amateurs). Some, such as Monte Major did not, at the time of printing, have good clubhouse facilities but the novelty and beauty of the course gives it, in our opinion, a good rating.

The choice might also differ from yours depending on the type of golf you enjoy. The author would be delighted to hear readers' opinions – email them to him at djwhyte@sol.co.uk.

1. PGA Golf De Catalunya (Catalonia)
2. El Saler (Valencia)
3. Golf Las Brisas (Costa Del Sol)
4. Sotogrande Old (Sotogrande)
5. Real Club De Golf Málaga (Costa Del Sol)
6. Torrequebrada Golf (Costa Del Sol)
7. Capdepera Golf (Mallorca)
8. Campo De Golf Villamartín (Alicante)
9. Golf Club Marbella (Costa Del Sol)
10. Montecastillo (Western Andalucía)
11. Santa María Golf & Country Club
12. San Roque Club (Sotogrande)
13. Son Muntaner (Mallorca)
14. La Cala Golf & Country Club R. Norte (Costa Del Sol)
15. Monte Mayor Golf (Costa Del Sol)
16. Club De Golf Cierro Grande
17. Golf & Country Club La Marquesa
18. Club De Golf Don Cayo

Below: Villamartín might be quirky and not up to modern standards, but many of its holes offer good tests.

Above: Sotogrande Old is an elegant course, rich in character and challenge.

Above: Son Muntaner is Mallorca's newest and one of its most entertaining courses.

Chapter 1

Catalonia

The region of Catalonia is now recognised as a self-determined and partly self-governing state within Spain. Its people are ambitious and hard-working and there is a gregarious buzz throughout the region. This has led to high standards in every aspect of life and a great appreciation for quality. In addition to Spanish, the independent Catalans speak their own language, Catalán, and have a passion for their native culture.

Golf has existed in Catalonia for many years, with the first club opening in 1914. Courses such as Costa Brava Golf Club, Pals and Real Golf El Prat were constructed in the 1950s and 1960s. There are nearly 30 18-hole layouts now available, along with several par 3 courses and a host of pitch and putt facilities. With this wide selection of courses, Catalonia is becoming increasingly popular for golfing holidays. It is also slightly cheaper to play golf here than in other parts of Spain.

A noticeable event for golf in the area was the opening in 1999 of the PGA's

Left: Tarragona became an important Roman military and political centre in the 3rd century BC. Above: Agua Blava, Costa Brava

superlative Golf de Catalunya course just south of Girona. This magnificent layout is destined to become one of Europe's top courses and will be a regular feature of the European Tour. The venue has provided a focus for the professional game in this part of Spain as well as a destination for visitors seeking a first-class course.

Catalonia's main airport is Barcelona and frequent flights from the UK can have you there in less than two hours from London airports. Several low-cost airlines and charters serve Barcelona flying from Stansted or Luton. Girona offers a good alternative for European flights, avoiding the two-hour drive from Barcelona to the northern part of the area. Catalonia has a good motorway system that is easy to navigate. Barcelona itself is the only potentially confusing spot for drivers, but signs are adequate and the motorway system relatively new and well planned.

The Catalonian weather is occasionally inclement from December through to February, but golfers from the north will find courses in good condition during this time. On most days temperatures reach 50 to 60°F, although it is occasionally cooler.

March to mid-May is the busiest period for golf throughout this region and it is important to reserve accommodation and tee times well in advance if you come at this time. During the height of summer especially inland, it can be humid and stifling, although cooling breezes along the coast make golfing conditions more bearable. Strong winds occur from time to time, most notably at La Tramontana, which can make it hard to play.

Barcelona

Barcelona is the capital of the region. It is considered to be Spain's most sophisticated city with an abundance of art and culture. Two thousand years of the area's history is presented in the city's museums, and its art galleries and theatres are rated among Europe's finest. Much of the celebrated Antoni Gaudí's architectural output is found in Barcelona. The flowing grandeur of his designs is free to be appreciated on many street corners and squares. Barcelona has a long association with opera and its focus is the famous and recently rebuilt Gran Teatre del Liceu on the Rambla. The medieval quarter, known as the Barri Gòtic, contains the Basilica of Santa Maria and the cathedral, which are also well worth seeing.

For night-time entertainment Barcelona caters for everyone's tastes with all sorts of nightclubs, restaurants and bars that often remain open until 04:00 or 05:00.

While the city is a focal point for non-golfing activity, there is also much for the tourist to appreciate in the rural hinterland. An excellent motorway system can take you into the countryside in a few minutes. There are also beach areas in nearby Stiges or Sant Pol de Mar that are easily reached by train from Barcelona. To the north lies the famous mountain and monastery of Montserrat.

As for golf, there are half a dozen courses in easy reach of central Barcelona, and courses in other parts of the province can be reached in a few hours.

Costa Brava

Situated north of Barcelona, the Costa Brava has long been a popular retreat, particularly with British tourists on budget package holidays. It is admired for its coastal resorts such as Tossa de Mar or Lloret de Mar. It also offers a more sophisticated, less tourist-oriented hinterland. Here are hidden farmhouses converted into exquisite restaurants and unique inns offering the highest standards of food and accommodation.

Below: La Sagrada Familia (Church of the Holy Family) in Barcelona is one of Gaudí's most famous works.

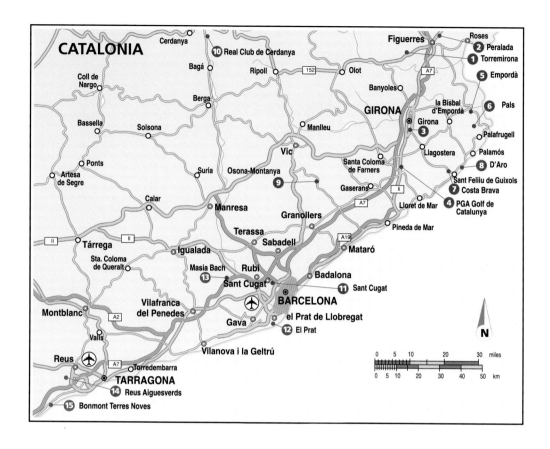

Costa Dorada

Along the coast are small, delightful coves while slightly inland there are unspoilt medieval villages set against the wonderful backdrop of the Alberés Mountains, part of the Pyrenees that divide Spain from France. The Salvador Dali museum, which is located in his birthplace town of Figueres, is a must for all visitors. The provincial capital of Girona is also worth making time for, with its remarkable old Jewish quarter and relaxed ambience.

Within the Costa Brava area there are eight courses to choose from, all of a very high standard. It is feasible to plan an entire golf vacation based in this area and indeed, given the standards of cuisine, accommodation and culture, it would be most recommended.

Costa Dorada

The Costa Dorada is situated south of Barcelona, and is also a popular holiday destination. There is not so much golf here in terms of numbers of courses on offer, but what there is surrounding the city of Tarragona will fulfil a week's stay with play on quality venues. Tarragona itself is a fascinating place to visit, particularly because of its many well-preseved Roman remains.

This area also offers recently built and more family-oriented tourist attractions such as Universal's Port Aventura, a sort of mini-Disney theme park near Salou. Costa Dorada also has a relatively unspoilt interior. Stepping into villages such as Montbrio del Camp is like stepping back in time.

1 Torremirona

Torremirona Golf Club, 17744 Navata, Catalonia
TEL: *972 56 67 00* **FAX:** *972 56 67 67*
WWW: *www.torremirona.com*
LOCATION: *138km from Barcelona and 25km from French border. 6km west from the A7 motorway (exit Figueres).*
COURSE: *18 holes, 5708m/6242yd, par 70, SSS 69*
GREEN FEES: *££££*
FACILITIES: *Clubhouse, changing room and showers, driving range, buggy hire, hand and electric trolley hire, pitching and putting greens, practice bunker, golf tuition, club repair, club rental, pro-shop, hotel, restaurant, bar, children's playground.*

Near the village of Figueres, the golf course surrounds a recently built hotel development. Hotel guests are offered special green fees on its course.

This course offers gently rolling fairways with only the occasional tree and several incidences of water coming into play. Play is often into the wind, which can make the holes seem much longer. The outward nine holes offer noticeable movement in the fairways. The back nine is flatter, although the real tests of this course are found here. The sting in the tail is concealed until the last three holes: the 16th is tight and requires a pinpoint accurate drive; the 17th is a dogleg right with strategic bunkering; nd it has an 18th on which all can go wrong on the approach, with a large lake to be negotiated on the right and fronting the green.

Bunker sand on this course tends to be heavy-grained, which does not make for good bunker play.

2 Peralada

Peralada Golf Club, 17491 Peralada (Girona), Catalonia
TEL: *972 53 83 06* **FAX:** *972 53 83 07*
LOCATION: *A7 motorway from Barcelona to exit 4. Follow signs for Llanca–Portbou and turn off for Peralada. The golf club is off to the right coming into town.*
COURSE: *18 holes, 6128m/6702yd, par 72, SSS 71*
GREEN FEES: *££*
FACILITIES: *Clubhouse, changing rooms and showers, driving range, buggy hire, hand and electric trolley hire, pitching and putting greens, practice bunker, golf tuition, club repair, club rental, pro-shop, restaurant, bar.*

This is a varied, rolling course in excellent condition. Set on broad, open slopes in the wide agricultural plain of Emporda country, it also offers one of the best clubhouse restaurants in the area. The view north to the Pyrenees is also remarkable.

The course from the visitors' tees measures 6128m (6702yd). This is not long but it brings out the best of the undulating land. With six teeing positions on each hole there are options for every level of player.

The course has a challenging and entertaining design along with a rustic feel. The most scenic section occurs at the confluence of the 4th, 5th, 6th and 7th. A variety of terrains influence play, with areas of thick cork trees, scrub oak and olive. Water is evident, with a river coming into play on at least five holes and ponds featuring near one or two greens. The tricky placement of bunkers calls for strategic positioning.

Above: The course at Peralada makes good use of the rolling landscape.

 # Girona

Girona Golf Club, 17080, Aparat de correus, 601, Girona, Catalonia
Tel: *972 17 16 41* **Fax:** *972 17 16 82*
Email: *golfgirona@infoservei.es*
Location: *A7 motorway exit 6.4km north of Girona. Autopista La Jonquer, direction of Banyoles.*
Course: *18 holes, 6100m/6671yd, par 72, SSS 72*
Green Fees: *££*
Facilities: *Clubhouse, driving range, buggy hire, hand trolley hire, pitching and putting greens, practice bunker, club rental, pro-shop, restaurant, bar, children's crèche, squash, fitness centre, sauna and showers.*

Above: Uphill and downhill drives are a common feature of Girona Golf Club, a course that is built through a tree-lined, rolling terrain that occasionally leaves awkward lies.

Girona, in spite of its historic centre, is a thoroughly modern town complete with hypermarkets and McDonalds. The entrance to Girona Golf Club was difficult to find from the A7 Autopista at the time of our visit, being on a rough track following a steep hill – this was surely due to be upgraded. Do not be put off, however, as there is a golfing paradise waiting on the other side.

The course is built through a greatly rolling terrain of densely wooded valleys which gives rise to sloping fairways and awkward lies. This can often seem unfair, as a well-struck drive will often roll into trouble. The par 5 9th is an example of this; a long dogleg left that falls away to the left. The green is situated on the opposite bank of the valley. It could be reached with two powerful blows, but drives often trickle left and result in a poor attacking position.

The course, which was designed by F.W. Hawtree, is sympathetic to its natural terrain and is a pleasant, but quite demanding, outing – the use of a buggy is highly recommended for anyone who is not completely fit. The movement in the course is also reflected on the greens. These slope or roll like a miniature version of their surrounds and make putting unpredictable.

4 *PGA Golf de Catalunya*

PGA Golf de Catalunya Carretera II, E-17455 Caldes
de Malavella, Girona, Catalonia
TEL: *972 47 25 77* **FAX:** *972 47 04 93*
LOCATION: *50 minutes drive from Barcelona. Exit 9
from A7 then off the N11 and follow signposts. From
Girona head south on N11 for 12km.*
COURSE: *18 holes, 6588m/7205yd, par 72,
SSS 72*
GREEN FEES: *££££*
FACILITIES: *Clubhouse, driving range, buggy hire,
hand trolley hire, pitching and putting greens, practice
bunker, club rental, pro-shop, restaurant, bar, changing
room and showers.*

PGA GOLF DE CATALUNYA

HOLE	YD	M	PAR	HOLE	YD	M	PAR
1	433	396	4	10	434	397	4
2	387	354	4	11	189	173	3
3	535	489	5	12	537	491	5
4	416	380	4	13	399	365	4
5	209	191	3	14	446	408	4
6	410	375	4	15	504	461	5
7	533	487	5	16	203	186	3
8	186	170	3	17	463	423	4
9	467	427	4	18	454	415	4
OUT	3575	3269	36	IN	3630	3319	36

7205YD • 6588M • PAR 72

Opened in June 1999, this is set to be the
premier course in Catalonia and indeed
probably one of the finest in Europe. A
further 18 holes are planned, along with a hotel
and real estate development, to further enhance
the facilities.

Built by the PGA European Tour after
nearly ten years of planning, the course
already feels mature and settled. In October
1999 it hosted the Gene Sarazen World Open
with great approval from tour professionals.

The setting is impressive – a distinctly
rolling track that rises and falls within a thick,
natural scrubland. The contrast between the
crisp fairways and
greens and
the broad expanse of wild woodland vegetation
is delightful. The short oak trees and thick
shrubbery should not come into play unless
you are extremely wayward. One or two
electricity pylons, although moved to have
minimum impact, are still an intrusion on this
lovely, natural amphitheatre. From several
points the Pyrenees and the more local
Montseny Mountains can be viewed away in
the distance.

The design has allowed for at least ten
downhill drives with only one noticeable climb
back, which was a good feat of routing. The
par 5 3rd is an example, an elevated tee
overlooking a well-
defined fairway that
terminates into a
lovely, buttressed
green which is
surrounded by
two lakes. The
first two shots
are important
on this hole in
order to be in
pitching distance
of a moated green.
There are further
lakes employed at the
11th and 13th.

Above: The design of Catalunya has allowed for at least ten downhill drives, with water featuring in the form of two large lakes and lovely buttressed greens.

Although the fairways are fairly generous, it is necessary to avoid the semi-rough and rough in order to cover the long distances. The best of players will love the challenge of this noble course. Most of us will find it rather severe, if only in length. Playing from the forward tees helps and there is no disgrace in moving up when you realise how stretching many of these holes can be.

The greens are absolutely impeccable and are an experience just in themselves. Given the challenges of the course, any player who is fortunate enough to come off with par

on a regular basis should feel justifiably proud of themselves.

The course is still relatively new. However, as the course settles it seems likely to develop into one of the best sporting tests in the whole of Europe. If its plans for further development turn into reality, Girona will become a notable golf destination in the near future.

Right: Catalunya's greens are varied and reflect their surrounding terrain. In spite of their newness, they are already fast and firm.

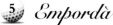 Empordà

*Empordà Golf Club, Ctra. de Palafrugell a Torroella,
17257 Gualta,Catalonia*
TEL: *972 76 04 50* **FAX:** *972 75 71 00*
WWW: *www.empordagolfclub.es*
EMAIL: *empordagolfclub@oem.es*
LOCATION: *A7 motorway Exit 6. Take the road from
Palafrugell to Torroella de Montgri. Then head off the
Motorway to Barcelona, and then towards La Bisbal.*
COURSE: *Green and Blue, 6170m/6747yd, par 71,
SSS 70*
GREEN FEES: *££££*
FACILITIES: *Clubhouse, driving range, buggy hire,
hand and electric trolley hire, pitching and putting greens,
practice bunker, golf tuition, club rental, pro-shop,
restaurant, bar, children's playground, showers.*

Inaugurated in 1991, this course is highly
rated. At present there are 27 holes, with
36 due for completion in 2001. There are
three sections – the Green, Blue and Yellow
(or Llevant, Gregal and Garbi – named for the
winds prevalent in the area). The Green and

*Below: The Blue course at Empordà is quite different from
this open 'links-like' Green course.*

Blue is the preferred combination, although
when the wind blows the two more sheltered
parkland sections are preferred.

The Green Course was designed by Robert
van Hagge as a 'Scottish links', although this
leaves a lot to the imagination. Distinct man-
made swells and extended bunkers characterize
this section along with tufts of rough that are
left intentionally high. The 6th on the Green, a
par 3, carries over an almost continuous bunker
of 140m/150yd.

The Blue and Yellow courses migrate into
thick, mature forest populated mainly with tall
Mediterranean pines, their long trunks topped
with thick 'umbrella' growth. The Blue course
is the more difficult and possibly the more
enjoyable. Its zenith is at the 6th and 7th holes,
both featuring the same large lake. The 6th
offers an option of some safety to the left with
a more daring, water-surrounded peninsula
directly towards the green. The 7th is a
mammoth par 5 with a medium carry over
water and an excellent shape throughout this
curving hole.

 Pals

Pals Golf Club, Ctra. de Pals-Playa de Pals, 17256 Pals, Catalonia
TEL: 972 63 60 06 **FAX:** 972 63 70 09
LOCATION: Pals is 40km from Figueres and found on the road from Pals to Playa de Pals.
COURSE: 18 holes, 6222m/6804yd, par 73, SSS 72
GREEN FEES: ££££
FACILITIES: Clubhouse, changing facilities and showers, driving range, covered driving range, buggy hire, hand trolley hire, pitching and putting greens, practice bunker, club repair, club rental, pro-shop, restaurant, bar.

Pals has long been a premier course in this part of the country, and its quality is reflected in its rather steep prices. The course is deliciously carved from a forest of tall, mature pines and the condition of all its aspects is exceptional.

The course extends towards the sea but this does not feature in any way. The heavily tree-lined avenues

Above: Umbrella pines are a shady but hazardous feature of Pals Golf Club.

create distinct enclosures to each hole, the playing of which calls for marked concentration. This has led to some criticism from players not used to such restricted driving conditions.

Pals demands a different approach off the tee and, when the appropriate adjustments have been made, it provides a delightful challenge. This is a course for the golfer who will stop and think about each shot even before reaching for a club.

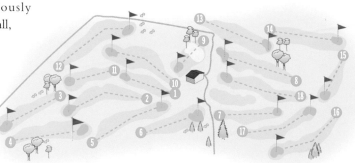

7 *Costa Brava*

Costa Brava Golf Club, 17246 Sta. Cristana d'Aro, Catalonia
TEL: *972 83 71 50* **FAX:** *972 83 72 72*
LOCATION: *100km from Barcelona on the A7 motorway. Take exit 9 for the town of Cristana d'Aro.*
COURSE: *18 holes, 5573m/6095yd, par 70, SSS 70*
GREEN FEES: *£££*
FACILITIES: *Clubhouse and showers, driving range, buggy hire, hand and electric trolley hire, pitching and putting greens, practice bunker, golf tuition, club repair, club rental, pro-shop, restaurant, bar.*

Set just a few miles inland from the bustle of this popular tourist coastal stretch, Costa Brava offers green avenues of tranquillity. The course is built around a large Catalan house of the 1840s and was opened in 1968. It is a tight proposition playing over

Below: The 18th hole at Costa Brava with its 19th-century clubhouse.

hilly ground, especially on the front nine with impinging cork oak and pine trees on both sides. These form a leafy hazard that must be avoided so choosing the driver every time can be folly. The fairways rise and dip quite noticeably so a variety of shots will be required.

The back nine holes call for a different game with longer and much more open holes. The contrast is welcome, although some might have preferred the more forgiving holes to be at the beginning of the round. Bunkering is large and ample, usually of a shallow low-lipped nature that presents little problem as long as you remember to splash out rather than thin the ball beyond its target.

During the week there is rarely a problem getting a round here, but weekends are very busy due to the large local membership and frequent competitions.

8 D'Aro

D'Aro Golf Club, 17250 Platja d'Aro, Catalonia
TEL: *972 82 69 00* **FAX:** *972 82 69 06*
LOCATION: *90km from Barcelona and 35km from Girona on the A7 motorway, exit 9.*
COURSE: *18 holes, 6004m/6566yd, par 72, SSS 71*
GREEN FEES: *££££*
FACILITIES: *Clubhouse, driving range, hand and electric trolley hire, putting green, golf tuition, club rental, caddy, pro-shop, restaurant, bar, sauna and showers.*

Overlooking the tourist resort of Platja d'Aro on the southern section of the Costa Brava, d'Aro is a difficult 18 holes along with a shorter nine-hole (par 27) section. The main course is tight, with ample cork oak and olive trees along with two sizeable lakes. Its mountainous location adds the further challenge of fairly uneven ground.

It might seem that everything is being thrown at the golfer here, with dastardly bunkering and elevated greens that are not easy to approach. On the positive side, the neighbouring Les Gavarres Mountains and surrounding scenery make for a wonderful setting that can go a long way to calming the nerves. If you can score here you will feel well rewarded.

SPEED OF PLAY

Golf's age-old tradition of courteous behaviour is under threat. This disquieting influence possibly comes from the number of new golfers taking up the game without the opportunity to learn proper etiquette. Speed of play is a contentious issue these days, particularly in high season, with so many mid to high handicappers clambering to get on to courses and taking four or five hours to get around. Conscientious clubs try to put low handicappers out early to keep up speed of play (and satisfy better golfers' needs), but this scheme is not practised everywhere.

---

9 Osona - Montanya

Osona-Montanya-El Brull Golf Club, 08553 El Brull Barcelona, Catalonia
TEL: *938 84 01 70* **FAX:** *938 84 04 07*
LOCATION: *From Barcelona, take the A7 motorway towards Girona, exit 14, N-152 towards Vic, turn off for Aiguafreda. Go through the village, turn right in the direction of El Montanya resort and follow the signs until you come to the club.*
COURSE: *18 holes, 5757m/6296yd, par 72, SSS 72*
GREEN FEES: *££££*
FACILITIES: *Clubhouse, sauna and showers, driving range, buggy hire, hand and electric trolley hire, putting green, practice bunker, golf tuition, club repair, club rental, pro-shop, restaurant, bar, swimming pool. Nearby riding stables.*

If you are based in Barcelona it is well worth making the trip out to this golf course. The foothill area of the Pyrenees is exceptionally charming with many ancient farm houses and medieval villages worth taking the time to explore. The town of Vic, set in the heart of the valley, is replete with excellent examples of ancient Spanish architecture. As an extra incentive, the Hotel Montanya offers discounts for guests wishing to play the course.

The course is set in a valley on the south side of a rich agricultural plain surrounded by mountains and is quite spectacular. The magnificent Montseny Mountain dominates the panorama.

The design of the course is quite simple, but it employs the natural features of its terrain as its main defence. The considerably sloping fairways make it play longer than it appears on the card. Add to this a fair number of trees, water hazards and sand, and Montanya becomes a testing little layout. The greens also incorporate noticeable borrows and bumps to make them much more demanding.

Osona-Montanya presents a naturally testing layout in a wonderful arena that is well worth making the effort to seek out.

10 *Real Club de Cerdanya*

Real Club de Cerdanya, 7520 Puigcerda, Girona
TEL: *972 14 14 08* **FAX:** *972 88 13 38*
LOCATION: *Near the border with France – take the N260 towards Puigcerda*
COURSE: *18 holes, 5886m/6437yd, par 71*
GREEN FEES: *£££*
FACILITIES: *Clubhouse, driving range, buggy hire, hand and electric trolley hire, putting green, practice bunker, golf tuition, club repair, club rental, pro-shop, restaurant, bar, swimming pool, hotel, sauna and showers.*

Above: Set in the Cerdanya Valley, Real Golf de Cerdanya presents a varied and picturesque challenge.

The little town of Puigcerda is in the heart of the Pyrenees. It might seem a bit out of the way for a game of golf but this is one of the most spectacular settings for any course and one that will reward those that take the time to venture there. The town is located in the Cerdanya valley with the River Segre flowing through and surrounded on all sides by breathtaking mountain peaks.

The course can be reached by road or rail – from Barcelona it is an easy two-hour drive north on the motorway. There also is a small airport with services from Barcelona. The course was built in the 1920s and has hosted many championships, although it might not reach the championship level of today's standards. Nevertheless, the course is favourable for low-handicap golfers who will relish its challenge.

All golfers will love the course's outstanding natural surrounds and incredible quality. There are elevated tees and greens with not too many bunkers (although those that there are can be punishing). There are a variety of tactical situations, making it a thinking golfer's course. The River Segre passing through the course adds to its charm and challenge.

The clubhouse has an excellent restaurant and there is a hotel attached. Chalets are also available and it would be possible to ski one day and golf the next.

11 Sant Cugat

*Sant Cugat Golf Club, 08190 Sant Cugat del Valles,
Barcelona, Catalonia*
TEL: *936 74 39 08* **FAX:** *936 75 51 52*
LOCATION: *Follow the E9 north from Barcelona*
COURSE: *18 holes, 5098m/5575yd, par 69,
SSS 68*
GREEN FEES: *££££*
FACILITIES: *Clubhouse, driving range, buggy hire,
hand and electric trolley hire, pitching and putting
greens, practice bunker, club repair, club rental, pro-
shop, restaurant, bar, swimming pool and showers.*

Situated north of Barcelona, Sant Cugat is
one of the oldest and best-known clubs
in the area. Its reputation comes from a
combination of setting and playability.

By the card it is short and, indeed, is an
easy length for any level of handicap. It also
appears hilly, but in practice is not too
strenuous. The charm of Sant Cugat is in
playing a course of manageable proportions
with many interesting elements to keep you
on your toes. Trouble comes in the form of
water, trees and bunkers, and these tighten a
relatively easy layout. Good drivers will be
tempted to go for the green from numerous
lofty prospects and, if you avoid the trouble,
these short par 4s can be terrific ego boosters.

12 El Prat

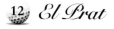

*El Prat Golf Club, Ctra. C246 Sitges–El Prat de
Llobregat 08820, Barcelona, Catalonia*
TEL: *933 79 02 78* **FAX:** *933 70 51 02*
LOCATION: *El Prat de Llobregat is around 20km
southwest from the centre of Barcelona.
Take the C246, towards Sitges and exit
towards the airport.*
COURSE: *18+9+9 holes, 6224m/6807yd, par 73,
SSS 73*
GREEN FEES: *£££££*
FACILITIES: *Clubhouse, driving range, buggy hire,
trolley hire, putting green, practice bunker, club repair,
club rental, pro-shop, restaurant, bar, changing rooms
and showers.*

El Prat is one of the foremost golfing
venues in Catalonia. Javier Arana was
responsible for the original layout and he has
designed a wonderful golf course in a natural
terrain with minimal environmental impact.
Situated next to the sea (and unfortunately
also to the airport), the course winds
picturesquely through pine forest and out on
to open links.

This golf course has 36 holes, which form
four possible rounds among pinewoods: Pink,
Blue, Yellow and Green. The Pink round is
the original one designed by Javier Arana.
The most recent round is the Blue one
designed by David Thomas. The Green and
Yellow rounds are a combination of the Blue
and the Pink ones. One of the most famous
is the Green, located on a plain among pine
trees and next to the sea, with many
bunkers. The Yellow round has more water
hazards and dangerous bunkers, especially at
the fairways.

The course opens out quite early on
from the trees onto a flat rolling terrain
interrupted by strategically placed palms and
plentiful bunkering. Good driving will leave
open approaches into large and billowing
greens of excellent quality and it is here you
can choose to 'bump and run' or pitch as
is appropriate. One thing to be wary of,
though, especially on the back nine, is the
effect of the wind. Even a mild breeze can alter
this course tremendously and clean
drives will find their way into the Bermuda
rough or worse and pitches can mysteriously
go astray and end in bunkers that should not
have been there.

El Prat is a highly rewarding course for
good golfers who will find every aspect of
their game being employed. An initial round
will reveal the subtle and often hidden
idiosyncrasies of the course, so it is worth
booking two rounds to fully appreciate the
wonderful layout.

13 Masia Bach

*Masia Bach Golf Club, Ctra de Martorell-Cadellades
E-08635 Sant Esteve Sesrovires, Barcelona*
TEL: *937 72 63 10* **FAX:** *937 72 63 56*
LOCATION: *Northwest of Barcelona, take the A2/A7
towards Tarragona. Take exit 25 for Martorell then
B224 to Capellades. The entrance is on the right.*
COURSE: *18+9 holes, 6271m/6858yd, par 72,
SSS 72*
GREEN FEES: *££££*
FACILITIES: *Clubhouse, driving range, buggy hire,
trolley hire, putting green, practice bunker, club repair,
club rental, pro-shop, restaurant, bar, changing rooms
and showers, indoor and outdoor swimming pools,
tennis court.*

This is a rugged course, with hazards such as rough ground, gullies, *barrancas* or dry river beds. A good course planner is therefore essential. Blind tee shots are common with bunkers being the best indication of direction, and a direct route over the hazards is often the best tactic. This is a 'risk-and-reward' course that may be enjoyed more the second time you play it.

Golf star José María Olazábal was responsible for many of the course's design features. Although it appears craggy and cantankerous, Masia Bach plays well. It is not quite as strenuous to walk as it appears and is generally enjoyable. The greens are receptively angled, usually quite long or wide and in good condition, making for challenging but exhilarating putting. Masia Bach also offers excellent practice facilities and a nine-hole course that is also well worth playing.

14 Reus Aiguesverds

*Reus Aiguesverds Golf Club, Ctra. De Cambrils s/n
(Mas Guardia), 43206 Reus, Catalonia*
TEL: *977 75 27 25* **FAX:** *977 75 19 38*
LOCATION: *On the Cambrills–Mas Guardia road.*
COURSE: *18 holes, 5944m/6500yd, par 72,
SSS 71*
GREEN FEES: *££*
FACILITIES: *Clubhouse, driving range, buggy
hire, hand and electric trolley hire, pitching and putting
greens, practice bunker, golf tuition, club repair, club
rental, pro-shop, restaurant, bar, changing rooms
and showers.*

Reus Aiguesverds Golf Club offers quite a flat, easy course apart from some stiff doglegs and a little water. It is becoming popular with British holidaymakers coming up from the nearby Salou area for a breath of fresh air and is ideal for senior golfers or high handicappers looking to enjoy a trouble-free round as long as they avoid the water.

The 5th is perhaps the most interesting hole, a long dogleg that leaves a firm second shot into a flat green with no bunkers. An over-ambitious shot could roll off a heavily cambered green. Trees are short and stocky but generally leave plenty of room on the fairways. The only real threat comes in the form of water at the 3rd, 9th and 13th, the last being perhaps the most difficult hole on the course. The water forces players to over-club and there is a long slipway to carry your ball further from the pin. The few bunkers that there are on the course tend to be large and flat.

*Above: Reus Aiguesverds is a relatively easy test apart from
the influence of some well-placed water hazards.*

15 🏌 *Bonmont Terres Noves*

Bonmont Terres Noves Golf Club, Urb. Terres Noves, 43300 Mont-Roig del Camp, Tarragona, Catalonia
TEL: *977 81 81 40* **FAX:** *977 81 81 46*
LOCATION: *From the A7 motorway, exit 38. Head north towards Mont-Roig, then left through the village then north again at signpost.*
COURSE: *18 holes, 6050m/6616yd, par 72, SSS 72*
GREEN FEES: *£££*
FACILITIES: *Clubhouse, driving range, buggy hire, hand trolley hire, pitching and putting greens, practice bunker, club repair, club rental, caddy, pro-shop, restaurant, bar, apartments, children's playground, swimming pool, tennis court and showers.*
VISITORS: *Handicap certificates are required.*

The Bonmont's impressive clubhouse is set in a wide area of almond and olive groves between the mountains and the Costa Dorada. The course is divided by the approach road to the clubhouse and is presented in two distinct halves. The front nine is graceful, fairly flat with wide flowing fairways and exquisite greens set against the grandeur of the mountains. Water forms green-front hazards on occasion. Two dried river beds dissect

Above: Dry river beds and a deep ravine dissect the course at Bonmont Terres Noves.

several holes and present great difficulty if you play into them.

The back nine appears gentle from the 10th, looking down towards the sea, but it is actually quite hard. Senior golfers may wish to hire a buggy for this half of the course as there are some steep uphill climbs. It is possible to do this at a slightly reduced cost.

The 15th, 16th and 17th play around a dramatic ravine with the 17th presenting the main difficulty. From the highest point of the course it is a long drive between the ravine and the scrub rough on the left. In terms of intimidation this prospect will shake the firmest composure. Wind is a frequent factor here, as on every aspect of this course, and there is not much shelter, making it a longer proposition than the 6050m/6616yd from the visitors' tees.

The club offers apartments and houses within the complex. These are of the highest standard at reasonable rates.

REGIONAL DIRECTORY

Where to Stay

Barcelona obviously offers the widest range and number of places to stay but it is not necessarily the golfing capital. Stay here if you are combining the delights of this extraordinary city, something that must be done, with golf in the half dozen or so courses on its doorstep.

Otherwise, Girona, the region's second city, and the many coastal resorts of the Costa Brava are ideal for golfing visitors. Most highly recommended is the five-star **Mas de Torrent** near Pals (972 30 32 92). This converted farmhouse hotel offers the highest standards, from its rustic rooms to the exquisite cuisine, along with several courses nearby. The **Parador Aigua Blava** is also well worth experiencing and offers good discounts at neighbouring courses. Its cliff-top setting is second to none and it's a treat to wander down to the harbour. The hotel is not luxury, more bijou/character and the price is to suit.

The following are other recommended hotels.

Park Hotel San Jorge. Calonge, Girona (972 65 23 11; Fax: 972 65 25 76).

Modern and comfortable, with a privileged location between two coves, surrounded by a pine tree park, which is part of this hotel. There is a pool that offers a beautiful view over the sea.

Allioli. Castello d'Empuries, Girona (972 25 03 00; Fax: 972 25 03 00).

A lovely 17th-century estate house only a short drive from France. Very well maintained and elegantly furnished in a classic style, with one of the most renowned restaurants in the area.

Grevol. Llanars, Girona (972 74 10 13; Fax: 972 74 10 87).

This retains all the style of the Central European hotels and is ideally situated for excursions and golf. There is bowling, snooker and a Jacuzzi in the hotel as well as other sports facilities.

The Hotel La Costa (349 72 66 77; www.grn.es/hlacosta) is a four-star hotel handy for Pals golf course.

Where to eat

Hispania (Barcelona) (937 91 04 57)

Authentic Catalan cuisine, which has won accolades from near and far. The classic *clam suquet*, similar to a fricassee, and the *crema catalana* (a rich caramel custard) are both delicious.

Torre del Remei (Girona) (972 14 01 82)

This stunning palace surrounded by gardens has been impeccably restored and now houses an elegant restaurant and hotel. The chef will delight you with his gourmet dishes and superb selection of wines.

El Bulli (Girona) (972 15 04 57)

Considered by many to be one of Spain's best restaurants and perhaps one of Europe's most beautiful, El Bulli is a must on any gourmet's itinerary. Expensive, but definitely worth the treat.

Below: Girona's ancient Jewish Quarter has a surprising number of elaborate gardens and courtyards.

Where to go

Tarragona. Six centuries as the Roman capital have left 'Tarraco' with a rich monumental heritage, including some of the best preserved remains of Roman architecture in Europe. The Amphitheatre, the Circus and the City Walls are very impressive and well worth visiting.

Delta Del Ebro. This 32,000-hectare area is one of the most important in Europe. It is home to more than 300 species of birds. The total number of birds ranges from 50,000–100,000 depending on the season. There is also an extensive flora with more than 500 different species.

Monasterios. This popular Cistercian Monastery Route includes the monasteries of Poblet, Santes Creus and Vallbona de les Monges. They were all founded in the 12th century and Poblet is today the largest active Cistercian monastery in Europe. These monasteries offer many fine examples of Gothic and Roman architecture.

Reus. This town offers very good shopping facilities in the old city centre, which is conveniently pedestrianized. Reus is also notable for its rich heritage of Modernist architecture. If you are interested in ballet, opera or classical music, an evening at the beautiful Fortuny Theatre is recommended.

Barcelona, a truly magnificent city, hosted the 1992 Olympic Games. You can visit the spectacular church *La Sagrada Familia*, designed by

Above: Masies de la Garrotxa, ancient homesteads in this once volcanic region.

famous architect Antoni Gaudí, stroll along the city's wide avenues, visit the numerous museums or just sit in a café and watch the world go by.

Catalonia Tourist Information Centre
Pg. De Gracia 107, 08008 Barcelona
Tel:+34 932 38 40 00
www.gencat.es/probert

Barcelona Tourism
Tel: +34 932 15 44 77
National and Local Police
Tel: 091/092

Official Golf Organisations
Catalan Golf Federation
Aribau, 282, 2nd 2eme, 08006 Barcelona
Tel: +34 934 14 52 62
Fax: +34 932 02 25 40

Association of Golf Clubs
Costa Brava-Girona
Apartat de correus 601
17080 Girona
Tel: +34 972 17 16 41
Fax: +34 972 17 16 82

Chapter 2

Valencia, Alicante & Murcia

As you move south through Catalonia and into Valencia (also known as the Levante – the East), the surrounding terrain gradually changes, the green treescapes of the northeast giving way to slightly drier conditions. This is an area of orange and lemon groves; the *huerta* or agricultural hinterland of Valencia is one of the richest farming regions in Spain. There are three main sections to this stretch of coast; the areas around the cities of Valencia and Alicante and the *comunidad autonoma* of Murcia. Each area has very good flight connections from Europe and different golfing conditions to offer.

The climate in this area is more predictable than it is in other parts of Spain. There is almost constant sunshine through most of the year and cooling sea breezes during the hottest spells. By mid-

February there is heat in the sun and ideal golfing conditions prevail into early May. October through to Christmas is also popular.

Valencia

If you are travelling south by car from Catalonia there are two golfing outposts that should be taken en route: Panorámica and Mediterráneo Golf Clubs. These are both north of Valencia. Otherwise, there are several spots around Valencia that would make an excellent golfing base. The world-famous El Saler golf course is a must for any golfer to this area. This is situated around 18km (11 miles) from Valencia Airport south of the *puerto*.

Apart from a nine-hole course at Manises near the airport, there are only two other courses around the city. Coupled with El Saler, these still make it worth stopping over for a few days. Valencia is a bustling metropolis and its excellent motorway

Left: Valencia Cathedral. Above: Panoramica's golf course is dotted with ancient farm structures.

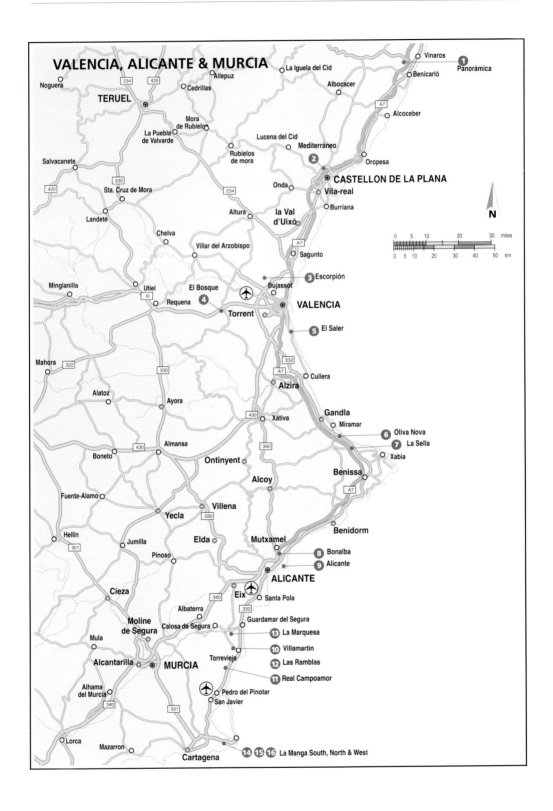

VALENCIA, ALICANTE & MURCIA

Noguera
Allepuz
La Iguela del Cid
Vinaros
1 Panorámica
Benicarló
234
420
Cedrillas
Albocacer

TERUEL
A7
Alcoceber

Mora de Rubielo
Lucena del Cid
La Puebla de Valvarde
Mediterráneo
Rubielos de mora
2
Oropesa
Salvacanete
Onda
CASTELLON DE LA PLANA
330
Sta. Cruz de Mora
234
Vila-real
420
Altura
la Val d'Uixó
Burriana
Landete
Chelva
Villar del Arzobispo
A7
Sagunto
Minglanilla
Utiel
El Bosque
Bujassot
3 Escorpión
III
Requena
4
VALENCIA
Torrent
5 El Saler
Mahora
322
330
332
A7
Cullera
Alatoz
Ayora
Alzira
430
Xátiva
Gandla
Miramar
6 Oliva Nova
Almansa
340
7 La Sella
Boneto
Ontinyent
Xabia
Fuente-Alamo
Alcoy
Benissa
430
A7
Villena
Hellin
Jumilla
330
Elda
Mutxamel
Benidorm
301
Pinoso
8 Bonalba
Yecla
9 Alicante
Cieza
ALICANTE
Albaterra
340
Eix
Santa Pola
Moline de Segura
Calosa de Segura
332
Guardamar del Segura
Mula
13 La Marquesa
Alcantarilla
Torrevieja
10 Villamartin
MURCIA
12 Las Ramblas
Alhama del Murcia
Pedro del Pinotar
11 Real Campoamor
340
331
San Javier
Lorca
Mazarron
14 **15** **16** La Manga South, North & West
Cartagena

N

0   5   10   20   30 miles

0 5 10   20   30   40   50 km

system will carry you to the inland courses with little bother. Prices compare favourably with most mainland courses. One bargain you might like to take advantage of is the large discount on green fees available if you stay at the Parador El Saler and play on that famous course. Visitors are usually delighted to discover this.

Valencia itself is an energetic and elegant city, particularly the *centro*. The architecture, especially the railway station (next to the Playa de Toros or Bullring) and the Town Hall, is particularly fine. 'Ciudad de las Artes y Ciencias' is the rather elaborate name for Valencia's newest attraction, an attempt no doubt to compete with Bilbao and Barcelona. Built on the former bed of the River Turia, it is an elaborate art, science and nature exposition.

Valencia is paella country, the region where, because of its rice production, the dish was invented. The most authentic versions of this popular Spanish dish are not found so much in Valencia itself but in the fabulous local restaurants in nearby villages, such as El Palmar, which is only 2km (1.4 miles) from El Saler golf course. Alicante also lays some claim to inventing paella, but their version is a seafood variety. The traditional 'Paella Valenciana' uses rabbit, chicken and snails along with rice and vegetables.

Alicante

Further south, Alicante is a busy tourist town popular with the Spanish as well as Northern European holidaymakers. Its long beaches, such as San Juan, are a tremendous lure, but they can get crowded. Golf courses are springing up everywhere around the city, partly to cash in on the massive tourist influx and also

to entice further housing and holiday apartment development. The results might not have the greatest aesthetic appeal but the courses are good nonetheless. It is outside the city, either inland or along the Costa Blanca, that you will find the best golf in the area with courses such as Villamartín, Bonalba and Campoamor gaining a good reputation.

Murcia

The relatively sleepy city of Murcia and its district of the same name do not have a wide choice of golf to offer. However, they do have one of the most famous golf resorts in Spain, La Manga. Set next to the popular Mar Menor, a beach area surrounding a wide, shallow lagoon, the surrounding high-rises are reminiscent of Miami Beach. La Manga is like a little piece of the British Isles, so popular that many UK and Irish golfers own property here. With the five-star Hyatt Regency Hotel at its heart, the resort also attracts American and European golfers onto its courses.

GOLF TUITION

Many tour operators offer the chance to attend a golf school in Spain, and these can be booked independently. There are several recommended centres. La Quinta Golf Club has a highly renowned golf academy directed by Manuel Piñero, one of Europe's top teaching professionals. La Quinta also offers Digital Swing Analysis using the PRO-GOLF© Dynamic Ruler© system. Islantilla Golf Resort has a professional, Macerana Tey, who is well known for her tuition of Spanish and other European golfers. The David Leadbetter Academy at La Cala Golf Resort in Mijas offers a complete range of golf lessons as part of its weekly and weekend packages.

Panorámica

Panorámica Golf Club, Urb. Panorámica, 12320
San Jorge, Valencia
TEL: *964 49 30 72* **FAX:** *964 49 30 63*
EMAIL: *panoramica@tsai.es*
LOCATION: *Off Motorway A7, exit 42 west towards
San Jorge.*
COURSE: *18 holes, 6037m/6602yd, par 72, SSS 72*
GREEN FEES: *£££*
FACILITIES: *Clubhouse, driving range, buggy hire,
hand and electric trolley hire, pitching and putting greens,
practice bunker, golf tuition, club repair, club rental, pro-
shop, restaurant, bar, changing room and showers.*
VISITORS: *Handicap required.*

Panorámica is part of a growing residential
and touristic development. The course's
growing reputation, especially in Germany
(thanks partly to the course designer,
Bernhard Langer), means that it can be busy
in the winter. Being the only course in this
area it is also popular with locals and is busy at
the weekends. After April it is much quieter.

Panorámica is not a difficult course, and
there is plenty of room on its wide, rolling
fairways, with little rough. Couples and high
handicappers will enjoy a game through the
olive trees, which do not present too much
obstruction. The course is still maturing and
new plantations do not feature as yet.

The 15th is a long hole, although only
Stroke Index 3. Surrounded by a sparse grove
of stubby olive trees, the terrain dips and rises
to the wide raised green.
It is not an easy
approach shot to judge.

The practice facilities
are good, with a large
driving range and the
Bernhard Langer Golf
School.

*Right: Bernhard Langer
designed the wide sweeping
holes of Panorámica.*

 # Mediterráneo

Mediterráneo Golf Club, Urb. La Coma, s/n 12190
Borriol, Valencia
TEL: *964 32 12 27* **FAX:** *964 32 13 57*
LOCATION: *In Borriol, next to the north exit of the
Motorway A7, 3.5km from Castellon*
COURSE: *18 holes, 6038m/6603yd, par 72,
SSS 72*
GREEN FEES: *£££*
FACILITIES: *Clubhouse, driving range, buggy hire,
hand trolley hire, pitching and putting greens, practice
bunker, golf tuition, club repair, club rental, pro-shop,
restaurant, bar, swimming pool, tennis court, squash,
fitness centre, showers and sauna.*

Just north of Castellon in Urbanización La
Coma, Mediterráneo is a pleasant course set
in a fairly varied wooded terrain. Pine trees
stand next to palms, with a few carob and
olive trees mixed in as well.

The course is surprisingly good, although
its reputation has not travelled far. Conditions
on the fairways and greens are excellent,
evidence either of high standards of
greenkeeping or a rich loam.

The distinctive 4th is the card-wrecker, a
515m/563yd par 5 with a huge carob tree
blocking the approach to the green. But the
green itself, well protected by bunkers and
with three tiers, is where the real action starts.
A combination of devious hazards and
deceptive putting surfaces makes Mediterráneo
a much more difficult test than you might first

expect. Golfers of all different levels will be surprised at the course's cunning and delighted with its condition.

 Escorpión

Escorpión Golf Club, Ctra. S. Ant. Benageber, Betera, Valencia
TEL: *961 60 12 11* **FAX:** *961 69 01 87*
EMAIL: *clubescorpion.com*
LOCATION: *Road to Ademuz, exit 11, towards Betera.*
COURSE: *18 holes, 6091m/6661yd, par 72, SSS 73*
GREEN FEES: *££££*
FACILITIES: *Clubhouse, driving range, buggy hire, hand and electric trolley hire, pitching and putting greens, practice bunker, club repair, club rental, pro-shop, restaurant, bar, swimming pool for members only, tennis court for members only and showers.*
VISITORS: *No visitors at weekends.*

Escorpión is a fairly basic member's club in the countryside surrounding Valencia. It is absolutely flat apart from a slight rise at the 18th and of a comfortable length, so it would not prove taxing for older or less experienced players.

The course starts with an interesting par 5. The hole is wide and accommodating, but a group of three or four trees block the approach to the 1st green. The 5th, 10th and 16th holes call for thoughtful strategies. The 18th hole is a more difficult par 5 slight dogleg of 546m/597yd. With ancient trees intruding sometimes well into the fairway, it is not an easy passage.

Above: The 18th at Escorpión is notable for its ancient gnarled olive trees.

El Bosque

El Bosque Golf Club, Ctra. Godelleta, km4100 46370 Chiva, Valencia
TEL: *961 80 41 42* **FAX:** *961 80 40 49*
EMAIL: *elbosque@xpress.es*
LOCATION: *4.1km from N3 Valencia Madrid exit 337.*
COURSE: *18 holes, 5915m/6469yd, par 72, SSS 72*
GREEN FEES: *££££*
FACILITIES: *Clubhouse, new two-tiered 35-bay driving range, buggy hire, hand trolley hire, pitching and putting greens, practice bunker, golf tuition, club repair, club rental, pro-shop, restaurant, bar, swimming pool, tennis court, showers, sauna and jacuzzi/spa.*

There are plenty of trees on this course but they are not too intrusive, just serving to define and tighten some of the holes. The terrain is rolling and occasionally hilly. The greens are interesting, in the classic butterfly shape that course designer Robert Trent Jones Senior is famous for. They tend to be difficult to read: try to put yourself into a pitching position for the flag with greens such as these. The 4th is a green hard to hold with a narrow entrance and strong bunkering in front. The 7th is another good test, a two-shotter on a par 5 if you get the right roll.

The back nine is the stronger, with at least six holes affected by water. The 13th is dangerous, as a good drive could go in the water, which is hidden out of sight. The 15th is a par 5 with no chance of hitting the green in two as it is very well bunkered. Overlooking the course there are apartments and villas that offer quite good value for families or small groups to rent.

 *El Saler*

El Saler Golf Club, Parador Nacional Luis Vives,
46012 El Saler, Valencia
TEL: *961 61 11 86* **FAX:** *961 62 70 16*
LOCATION: *From Valencia follow signs for Valencia*
Port Saler. Entrance vaguely signposted Parador
Nacional Luis Vives
COURSE: *18 holes, 6355m/6950yd, par 72, SSS 73*
GREEN FEES: *££££ (Green fees reduced significantly*
for guests at the Parador El Saler).
FACILITIES: *Clubhouse, driving range, covered driving*
range, buggy hire, hand trolley hire, pitching and 3
putting greens, practice bunker, golf tuition, club repair,
club rental, caddy, pro-shop, restaurant, bar, changing
room and showers.

EL SALER							
HOLE	YD	M	PAR	HOLE	YD	M	PAR
1	428	391	4	10	399	365	4
2	376	344	4	11	568	519	5
3	531	486	5	12	198	181	3
4	189	173	3	13	348	318	4
5	515	471	5	14	413	378	4
6	442	404	4	15	564	516	5
7	356	327	4	16	426	390	4
8	359	328	4	17	213	195	3
9	156	143	3	18	466	426	4
OUT	3354	3067	36	IN	3596	3288	36

6950YD • 6355M • PAR 72

El Saler is perhaps the nearest that Spain has to a links course. One of the best courses of its type in the country, it makes the most of the land it is built through. To call it a links is perhaps slightly misleading when the majority of holes play through pine forest. Nevertheless, the sandy subsoil and undulating terrain with several holes opening onto the dunes make for varied and exciting golfing conditions.

The course surrounds a somewhat bedraggled clubhouse as well as the Parador de El Saler, the ideal place to stay and play this course. The 1st, 9th and 18th holes are on the hotel's doorstep. The first four holes play inland through pine woods. They serve as a good introduction to the course's playing conditions. A notable feature is the soft, sandy wasteland that lines most holes. Coupled with the vegetation – consisting of myrtle and mimosa bushes as well as the succulent 'Cats Claws' – this fairway perimeter is an area you do not wish to stray into. The soft, powdery sand is very difficult to play from.

The 5th is a long par 5 of 451m/493yd doglegging slightly right and blind off the tee. The entrance to the green is well bunkered and it is backed by tall dunes. The 6th, 7th and 8th play over similar land before turning back to the clubhouse at the 9th. The 9th hole is a delightful par 3 with a view of the Parador swimming pool.

The 10th to the 16th play inland. There is evidence of links throughout, although mainly lined with pine trees and bushes. The 17th and 18th return to the dunes. The 17th is a long par 3 that can be difficult even without a wind. The 18th doglegs left along high dunes. With a good drive you are looking into the green below, well bunkered but welcoming a great final approach.

Above: The sandy wastes and troublesome vegetation of El Saler's 17th green.

Below: The 18th green with Parador El Saler in the background.

Oliva Nova

 ## La Sella

Oliva Nova Golf Club, 46780 Oliva, Valencia,
TEL: *962 85 59 75* **FAX:** *965 78 07 66*
WWW: *www.Chg.es*
EMAIL: *ngerman@Chg.es*
LOCATION: *N332, 4km south of Oliva in the direction of Alicante at bridge signposted Club de Golf Oliva Nova (Camspa just after).*
COURSE: *18 holes, 5832m/6378yd, par 72, SSS 72*
GREEN FEES: *£££*
FACILITIES: *Hotel, clubhouse, covered driving range, buggy hire, hand trolley hire, pitching and putting greens, practice bunker, golf tuition, club repair, club rental, pro-shop, bar, tennis court and showers.*

Oliva is an excellent club golfers' course – flat, easy to get around and fair. There is plenty of well-placed water, but the course does not have hidden tricks, leading to a satisfying round if you play well enough.

There are often several ways to play each hole – a factor attributed to the course's enigmatic designer, Seve Ballesteros. He has turned a relatively flat terrain into an exciting golf course. The length and pace of the holes have you clubbing with every option, again a feature of clever design.

The 6th is a demanding long par 3 with a big bunker on the left and a ditch in front. At the 8th, a reasonable par 5, beware of water front and right of the green. The 15th is the toughest hole on the course, a long par 4 with water creeping on the left. A good drive that clears the left bunker will be the best method to attack the green, but aim at the right half to avoid the lake.

La Sella Golf Club, 03749 Jesus Pobre, Valencia,
TEL: *966 45 42 52* **FAX:** *966 45 42 01*
EMAIL: *lasella@arrakis.es*
LOCATION: *Denia, La Xara, signposted.*
COURSE: *18 holes, 5919m/6473yd, par 72, SSS 71*
GREEN FEES: *££ book in advance*
FACILITIES: *Apartment-hotel, clubhouse, driving range, buggy hire, hand and electric trolley hire, pitching and putting greens, practice bunker, club rental, pro-shop, restaurant, bar, showers and sauna.*

If you can find your way into La Sella through the burgeoning development of hillside villas you will find a delightful course. José María Olazábal advised on the course's design and has produced an exciting layout. Set within a valley with a variety of trees lining most fairways, the course presents some excellent driving situations and fast greens.

The 6th hole is most memorable, with a shoot of trees leading to a narrow fairway. The front nine here is as good as you could wish for, being both sporty and picturesque.

The back nine is newer and more open, with fine views of the nearby mountains. Almond, orange and grapefruit trees line the fairways and players are welcome to pick the fruit from the trees. The surrounding terrain can cause peculiar playing conditions in the warmer months, when hot winds blow up in the afternoon and play havoc on the course. Through January and February this is replaced by a cold wind that can be equally disruptive.

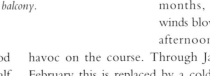
Above: The view of Oliva Nova from the clubhouse's balcony.

Bonalba

Bonalba Golf Club, 03110 Muchamiel, Valencia
TEL: 965 97 05 11 **FAX:** 965 96 05 05
LOCATION: A7 – Alicante–Valencia, exit 67 and signposted.
COURSE: 18 holes, 6367m/6963yd, par 72, SSS 72
GREEN FEES: ££
FACILITIES: Paddle courts, clubhouse, driving range, buggy hire, hand and electric trolley hire, putting green, golf tuition, club repair, club rental, pro-shop, restaurant, bar, tennis court and showers.

This course is a little exposed, especially on the back nine, but this probably adds to its 'big-hitter' appeal. From the tees it can be long and testing, but there is a diversity of holes that keeps the course exciting. Each hole presents a different characteristic. The front nine is more European with lakes, trees and flowers, whereas the back nine is more spartan with highs and lows and interesting views. Tree plantations will add to the course's appeal as they mature and come more into play.

The 5th is a par 5 that is reachable in two, but a lake in front of the green makes you think twice. The 7th is the most difficut hole. It is long but impossible to take a driver off the tee with a lateral water hazard ahead. Use a 3-iron for 183m/200yd and another onto the green.

Bonalba's greens can be fast, especially on the back nine. Although from the back this can be a tester, there are good forward tee options allowing everyone a pleasant round of golf to suit them.

Alicante

Alicante Golf Club, 03540 Alicante, Valencia
TEL: 965 15 37 94 **FAX:** 965 16 37 07
LOCATION: A7, exit towards Playa de San Juan or N340 road, towards Alicante. The course is signposted and just at the back of San Juan.
COURSE: 18 holes, 6245m/6830yd, par 72, SSS 73
GREEN FEES : £££
FACILITIES: Clubhouse, driving range, buggy hire, hand trolley hire, putting green, practice bunker, golf tuition, club repair, club rental, pro-shop, restaurant, bar, tennis court, squash and social club.

Just at the back of San Juan, a busy tourist area, a new swathe of tourist development is under construction. On our visit the area immediately surrounding the golf course was dominated by cranes. This will now be a complex of apartments and villas.

This course is very good. Designed by Seve Ballesteros and opened in 1997, it is in fine condition and a demanding test. The 2nd and 3rd holes are the most beautiful. The 3rd is a very short par 3 that gathers the water from a long waterfall before it. With added bunkers it could spell disaster. The other par 3s are quite long, apart from the 12th.

The course is quite flat and an easy walk. With lots of water at the 17th and 18th these two could ruin a good round. The course is a typical Seve design – long carries off the tee with lakes and out of bounds. The greens are true and testing, making it all the harder to save par. There are some pleasant views of the far-off mountains.

Above: Alicante Golf Club is an island of green in the middle of an expanding, built-up tourist area. Despite the development, the course is particularly good.

Villamartín

Villamartín Golf Club, Ctra. Cartagena-Alicante, km 7,600, 03189 Orihuela, Valencia
TEL: *966 76 51 60* **FAX:** *966 76 51 58*
LOCATION: *From Torrevieja towards Cartagena on the N332 coastal route, turn off towards Torrevieja.*
COURSE: *18 holes, 6132m/6706yd, par 72, SSS 72*
GREEN FEES: *£££*
FACILITIES: *Clubhouse, driving range, buggy hire, hand and electric trolley hire, putting green, practice bunker, golf classes, club rental, pro-shop, restaurant, bar.*

This course has more of a classic layout than you tend to meet in the area. It is not particularly long but wonderful to play. Villamartín has been established for nearly 30 years. On the downside, its facilities are surprisingly run-down, the pathways from green to tee quite rough and the golf services almost non-existent. However, the overall character of the course overcomes any quibbles about the peripheries.

Many holes require a drive and wedge, but both shots must be accurate. The greens are beautiful, generally large and a joy to roll over. The 9th plays over a frog pond with swallows swooping to catch flies. The 14th is a remarkable par 5 with two canyons to carry. The 17th is a long par 3 well over 200m/219yd from an elevated green across a valley to a small green – a demanding prospect.

There is a good rhythm to the types of holes here, with a pleasant balance of quiet, tree-lined fairways and then onto more dangerous terrain. Apart from the ancient buggies and cart paths that are rough and dusty, players who know a good course when they play one will enjoy Villamartín's classic golf atmosphere.

Below: The par 3 9th at Villamartín plays over a pond with swooping swallows.

Real Campoamor

Real Campoamor Golf Club, Ctra. Cartagena-
Torrevieja, km48, 03189 Orihuela, Valencia
TEL: 965 32 13 66 **FAX:** 965 32 24 54
LOCATION: Road N-332 Cartagena-Alicante. Well
signposted on highway.
COURSE: 18 holes, 6203m/6784yd, par 72, SSS 73
GREEN FEES: £££
FACILITIES: Clubhouse, driving range, buggy hire,
hand and electric trolley hire, pitching and putting greens,
practice bunker, golf tuition, club repair, club rental, pro-
shop, restaurant, bar and showers.

This is a visitor-friendly club with
excellent facilities. Real Campoamor's
brand new clubhouse perched on the highest
point of the property offers inspirational
views. The course is comfortable for every
level of player; with wide-open fairways and a
dearth of hazards even beginners will not feel
intimidated.

Awkward lies are the most common
difficulty that you will encounter. The course
flows over rolling terrain so you are usually
playing up or downhill. Thankfully, however,

*Above: Real Campoamor is a comfortable course for every
level of player. Fairways are generous and hazards few,
giving players an opportunity to relax.*

this does not include sideways-tilted fairways.
A variety of trees line most holes and help to
define them. Apart from this there is plenty of
room, so a misdirected shot will be punished
but rarely lost.

Raised greens are another regular feature on
this course. There is a stiff rise at the 7th,
which is a difficult par 5. The best advice is to
play for position on this and the rest of the
back nine. The fairways tend to be long and
curving with several blind tee shots to
negotiate. The best hole is probably the 3rd, a
par 4 that is long from the tee, driving
between two big cypress trees that are barely
ten metres apart. The second shot (if you've
got one) is a downhill carry to a bunker-
surrounded green. The 8th hole is another
good drive from a high tee, with an excellent
view of the fairway.

12 *Las Ramblas*

*Golf Club Las Ramblas, Crt Alicante Cartagena,
km48, 03189 Orihuela, Valencia*
TEL: *965 32 20 11* **FAX:** *965 32 21 59*
EMAIL: *enavarretes.profotur@nexo.es*
LOCATION: *Just off the N332, towards Cartagena and
well signposted.*
COURSE: *18 holes, 5770m/6310yd, par 72, SSS 71*
GREEN FEES: *££+*
FACILITIES: *Clubhouse, driving range, buggy hire,
hand trolley hire, pitching and putting greens, practice
bunker, golf tuition, club repair, club rental, pro-shop,
restaurant, bar, swimming pool, tennis court, squash,
fitness centre, showers and sauna.*

Whoever decided to build a golf course through this tract of land must have been imaginative. Las Ramblas works remarkably well and offers a completely different test from its neighbours. It has a complicated layout that rambles through humps, hillocks, deep ravines and rocky canyons with lots of trees and, so as not to be too lenient, a lake. Coupled with tiny greens this course is a nightmare for beginners and the impetuous, so the best way to approach Las Ramblas is simply to have fun. Having said that, there is generally a safe route to most holes. Many are quite short so par or even birdie is not impossible – if you can find your way to the fairways and greens. Blind tee shots are always irksome, though, and there are a few of these.

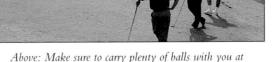

*Above: Make sure to carry plenty of balls with you at
Las Ramblas.*

The 7th is an incredible dogleg par 4 over a deep canyon and onto a raised green. Here, like most other holes, you have to place each shot with absolute precision. Players that do so will begin to warm to this type of game. The 10th is the most difficult par 3 to a small green with wind often blowing through the canyon between. The 17th is the longest par 4 but is more open. Las Ramblas is no walk-in-the-park, it is more of a ramble or scramble through the woods. You will either hate it or love it – depending on how you play it.

13 *La Marquesa*

*La Marquesa Golf Club, Ciudad Quesada II, 03170
Rojales, Valencia*
TEL: *966 71 42 58* **FAX:** *966 71 42 67*
LOCATION: *Towards Cartagena on N332, 6km from
Guardamar and 10km from Torrevieja.*
COURSE: *18 holes, 5747m/6285yd, par 72,
SSS 70*
GREEN FEES: *££*
FACILITIES: *Clubhouse, driving range, covered driving
range, buggy hire, hand trolley hire, pitching and putting
greens, practice bunker, golf tuition, club repair, club
rental, pro-shop, restaurant and bar.*

La Marquesa is set on a valley floor and despite dry-looking surrounds and palm trees, its first four holes route over marshland so it can be wet in winter. The rest of the course is good. Generally it is flat, and with the well-irrigated location usually in first-class condition.

Water comes in on several occasions, but judicious play will avoid it. The layout tends to favour mid to high handicappers – better golfers might find it pedestrian. Most of the year it plays well and most golfers find its sheltered location pleasant.

14 *La Manga South*

La Manga, South course, La Manga Club – Los Belones, 30385, Los Belones, Murcia
TEL: *968 13 72 34* **FAX:** *968 15 72 72*
LOCATION: *Towards La Manga del Mar Menor on the N331 and signposted to the right.*
COURSE: *18 holes, 6361m/6956yd, par 71, SSS 69*
GREEN FEES: *£££*
FACILITIES: *Clubhouse, driving range, buggy hire, hand and electric trolley hire, pitching and putting greens, practice bunker, golf tuition, club repair, club rental, pro-shop, restaurant and bar.*

Even from the visitor's tees La Manga's South course feels lengthy. After a few rounds you might learn the best lines to take off corners and gain best approach positions, but initially it seems to play much longer than its 6361m/6956yd. Arnold Palmer improved the course in the early 1990s, trying to bring charm to a rather flat and trying tract.

For the long driver, this course can be a treat. There are many times where a sound drive of 225m/246yd-plus will allow a decent approach shot to the green over huge bunkers, *barrancas*, dry river beds or lakes.

At the 15th, a *barranca* extends down the left of this long fairway, then cuts across in front of the green, making it a par 4 of 386m/422yd. The final four holes make for a testing finish. The Par 3 17th is, like them all, long and well bunkered with a wide carry over water while the 18th, the signature par 5, holds hidden dangers. A pond is visible to the left but there is a second pond hidden to the right. With a large cross-bunker, the average golfer plays safe to it then lays up before the wide *barrancas* before the green. The green is well bunkered and requires a confident strike where the back of the green is safest. The wind tends to get up in the afternoon and makes the back nine holes more difficult.

15 *La Manga North*

La Manga Club – Los Belones, 30385, Los Belones, Murcia
TEL: *968 13 72 34* **FAX:** *968 15 72 72*
LOCATION: *As La Manga South.*
COURSE: *18 holes, 5518m/6034yd, par 72, SSS 71*
GREEN FEES: *£££*
FACILITIES: *As for La Manga South.*

The North Course, which has just been given a major facelift, is more undulating than the South and offers a different, yet no less challenging round of golf. Relying on precision rather than length, an added challenge is provided by the many *barrancas* that snake their way through the course. These natural gullies can wreck a scorecard. The 11th, for instance, is crossed by a *barranca* at 174m/190yd from the tee. It takes a confident driver to clear this channel but the psychological factor sees many good golfers falling short. Water is a prominent feature, particularly on the back nine.

Above: The putting course at La Manga is just one of the many extra facilities offered at this comprehensive resort.

16 *La Manga West*

La Manga Club – Los Belones, 30385, Los Belones, Murcia
TEL: *968 13 72 34* **FAX:** *968 15 72 72*
LOCATION: *As for La Manga South.*
COURSE: *18 holes, 5680m/6212yd, par 73, SSS 71*
GREEN FEES: *£££*
FACILITIES: *As for La Manga South.*

It is surprising how many golfers elect the West Course as their favourite. This course was opened in 1992. It was designed by Dave Thomas through undulating pine woodland. It is very tight and twisting, especially on the front nine, so there is little room for error. This is the case at the 1st hole, where a wide lake sits just before the green.

Club selection and confident striking are demanded at the earliest stage and continue throughout the round. The West Course is much shorter than the South Course but demands more concentration and consideration for every shot.

Blind holes come into play on the back nine on a hilly terrain, which can be frustrating for the first time out. The 18th is anything but blind; it is a high tee perched on a rocky prominence looking over the resort as well as its fairway and green. A good drive here could make up for the frustrations off the tee of previous holes.

If you are hitting straight on the West Course and club only according to the distance required off the tee, there is a strong chance of coming off with a good score. But mistakes will be paid for dearly and until you are familiar with the layout, they will be hard to avoid. In spite of the course's shorter length, it is still a demanding test, even for better golfers. Most players come off the course charmed by its intricacies and its lovely views.

LA MANGA CLUB

Built in the early 1970s, La Manga is advertised as 'A Golfer's Paradise' in an ideal, year-round climate. This well-established sports and leisure resort located near the Cabo de Palos, 48km from Murcia, is particularly well promoted and patronised by golfers from the UK.

Some of the original facilities are now dated, although there is a programme in place to keep the resort up to date. New developments, such as the excellent self-catering Peninsular Club or the five-star Hyatt Regency Hotel, offer exceptional standards of accommodation. The surrounding hills are also dotted with villas and apartments owned or rented by the legions of La Manga followers who come year after year or who have chosen to retire here.

La Manga is effectively a self-contained town with many facilities within its 1,400 acres. There are shops, supermarkets, a petrol station, casino, tennis academy, soccer school, a children's activity centre, swimming pools and an excellent putting course. There are restaurants and bars offering everything from elegant, sophisticated eating to burgers. Nearby on the Mar Menor is a watersports centre. There also is a diving school attached to the resort.

REGIONAL DIRECTORY

Where To Stay

In the Valencia area the **Parador de El Saler** (961 61 11 86) is a must for all golfers. The rooms are excellent although there is a slight holiday-camp ambience and the pool area needs upgrading. The price of lodging is reasonable, but it is the 18 holes of El Saler golf course surrounding you and the fact that you pay almost a quarter of the usual green fee by staying in the Parador that makes it irresistible.

Only a couple of kilometres along the beach is **Hotel Sidi Saler** (961 61 04 11) the only practical alternative to the Parador. This is a five-star establishment built 25 years ago. It is rather dated in decor but used to looking after golfers. It runs a regular shuttle service into the centre of Valencia.

Oliva Nova Beach and Golf Hotel is south of Valencia near the coast (962 85 33 00). It overlooks the golf course and is well appointed. There are good restaurants in and nearby the resort.

Alicante is a maze of high-rise holiday apartments but you do find the occasional hotel. The **Holiday Inn** in San Juan (965 15 61 85) is basic but efficient and minutes from Alicante Golf Club.

If you are going to stay in **La Manga Club** (968 13 72 34) you have probably booked well in advance through your local tour operator. Everything you need is there, so plan to escape from the world for three or four days and play all the courses. The Peninsular Club offers highly recommended self-catering studios with its own pool, snack bars and restaurants.

Where to Eat

El Palmar near El Saler must have some 24 family-run restaurants in a tiny village and the best paella in Spain. The **Establishment** seems to be one of the best eateries with views over l'Albufera lake but there are plenty of others to choose from. The **Parador de El Saler** restaurant is very passable, serving local dishes with excellent appetisers. The menu does not alter from lunch to dinner nor throughout the week. Near El Bosque Golf Club in the village of Chiva is the **Restaurant Peligri** – ask for directions from the golf club as it is somewhat difficult to find.

Alicante is known for its seafood paella. **El Patio de San Juan** (965 65 68 00) is one of the best known in the tourist sector of San Juan. Outside Alicante, look for **Venta la Montana** (965 88 51 41), a charming mountain hostel with antique farming implements hung on the walls and traditional 'country' dishes served. **La Manga** has several good restaurants on the property or in the Hyatt Regency Hotel. For something more simple there are one or two local establishments just off the resort.

Where to Go

The coast between Valencia and Alicante is renowned for beach holidays with hedonistic hot spots such as **Benidorm** included. It is all a bit frenzied, but there are a few quiet coves yet to be discovered. Get your tan by the hotel pool and on the golf course. Otherwise head for the city of Valencia into its **'zone historic'** for shopping and various styles of architecture. Driving and parking in the designated underground city car parks makes this quite easy, although some hotels offer a shuttle bus service. La Seo with its Gothic tower is a Valencian landmark. The city's cathedral was founded in 1262 and has grown in stages, each with its own distinct style. La Lonja is an incredible 15th-century hall that hosts concerts and exhibitions. Go if there is something on, just to experience the atmosphere in this cavernous space. **Ciudad de las Artes y Ciencias** is the rather elaborate name for Valencia's newest attraction, which, when complete, will be an Art, Science and Nature display.

The busy port town of **Alicante** is given over to domestic tourism along its beach front, although the city is quite elegant with lots of outdoor cafes. The cliff-top **Castillo de Santa Bárbara** and the **Barrio de Cruz** on the same site are worth exploring and offer excellent views. The **Esplanada de España**, a palm-lined promenade merits a languid evening stroll.

Near La Manga, the **Mar Menor**, a shallow lagoon separated from the Mediterranean by a sand bar that now supports various high-rise apartment blocks, is a busy watersports resort with the water temperature usually warmer than the sea.

The city of **Murcia** is pleasantly prosperous and its centre is a welcome change from the busier tourist spots.

Tourist Information Offices
Alicante Tourist Information Centre,
Esplanada de España, 2–03002
Tel: 965 20 00 00

Castellon Tourist Information Centre,
Pza, María Agustina, 5 – 12003
Tel: 964 22 10 00

Valencia Tourist Information Centre,
Pza, 48 – 46002
Tel: 963 94 22 22

Chapter 3

Eastern Andalucía

Andalucía is Spain's largest region. It has a population of six million people spread over eight provinces. From the desert-like Almería to the Huelva area on the border with Portugal, the region extends 2000km (1200 miles). Within it is Spain's most popular destination for golf, the Costa del Sol.

Each year golfers from Northern Europe and other parts of the world come here to enjoy warm weather, excellent courses and a relaxed ambience. The Costa del Sol is also strongly associated with cheap package holidays that are particularly attractive to British visitors. With great improvements in both the infrastructure and the standard of amenities in the coastal resorts, there is now a more sophisticated feel to the Costa del Sol.

Left: Monte Mayor plays through one of the most unlikely golf terrains. Above: Mijas is perhaps the most popular of Spain's golf resorts.

Digging a little deeper into Andalucía's character, you will find a region of great cultural diversity. Many of Spain's most enduring national symbols and traditions originated here, including flamenco, fiestas, tapas bars, bullfighting and sherry. The region is renowned for its vibrant art, Moorish architecture and wildlife parks. Although a marvellous sunny climate prevails along the coast all the year round, it is also possible to ski in the Sierra Nevada mountain range for much of the year.

From the east, Andalucía commences with the Costa del Almería. This area has only just started developing a tourist industry, with two main centres at Roquetas de Mar and Mojacar. These are pleasant conurbations, although still in the process of development. The coastline is rocky with charming, unspoilt bays. The region's interior by contrast is rather stark, a sun-seared desert landscape that the Italian film industry found an ideal location in which to film its Spaghetti Westerns. Acres of canvas-covered fields produce succulent tomatoes and melons in abundance, sheltered from the strong, warm winds that continually sweep the area from the south.

In golfing terms, there are several good facilities that are gaining in popularity through the spring, autumn and winter months. The courses are found down by the coast, somewhat protected from the stronger inland winds. The area becomes very hot in July and August (30°C+). The coastal drive from Almería towards Málaga is worthwhile as opposed to the slightly faster inland toll road.

The N340

A word of warning is required regarding the N340 dual-carriageway between Málaga and the Sotogrande area. Although there is now a new stretch of excellent *autopista*, the N340 is still the main service route for many of the resort areas and golf facilities. Following the coast, it twists and turns dramatically in places. Local drivers are used to this, so the average speed of traffic is fast. Newcomers find it frightening – and, indeed, there are frequent accidents.

Costa del Sol

Between Málaga and Marbella is a 30-mile coastal strip that has become synonymous with 'sun and fun' holidays. Torremolinos was the first community to be caught up in the tourist boom of the 1950s, with neighbouring fishing towns soon to follow. As the Costa del Sol developed, it became a little indifferent to its many enthusiasts and there was a drop in standards while prices rose, particularly in the late 1980s. In the face of decreasing tourist numbers this trend was arrested. Now you will find a much-improved region that again offers high standards.

With 300 days of sunshine per year and nearly 60 golf courses available, golfers find no end of opportunities on the Costa del Sol. However, the Costa's popularity has meant that there has been increasing pressure on the courses during their busiest times.

The Marbella Area

This is the epicentre of the Costa del Golf: there are around 30 courses between Málaga and the west side of Marbella. A few are oriented towards a private membership, but almost all of them welcome visitors.

First-time golfers to the area may have a problem finding courses such as Guadalhorce, Torrequebrada, Santa María and Golf Club Marbella. Aloha, Monte Mayor, El Paraíso and Los Arqueros are also somewhat difficult to find, lacking clear and precise directions. Signs are posted along the N340, but often simply state *Campo de Golf* and do not indicate which one. It is worth bearing in mind that during the busy golfing season those who arrive late for their tee times may be unable to find an alternative time to play. Plan accordingly and obtain clear directions to the course, perhaps from your hotel staff. Most of all, allow yourself plenty of time to reach the course. If you are early you can always warm up with a bucket of balls before your round.

When to Play

The season in this area picks up around mid-September and is busy from mid-February until the end of April. The courses are not overly crowded in May

and September. During the summer, the best times to play golf are early in the morning or after 17:00.

New Developments

New courses are opening all along the Costa del Sol, such as the Dave Thomas-designed Marbella Club Golf Resort. It nestles in the mountains near Monte Mayor. A new road has been laid that meanders its way through the hills to the resort. This new complex is owned by a hotel and leisure group that controls three of the most luxurious hotels on the Costa del Sol: Hotel Torrequebrada, The Marbella Club and Hotel Puente Romano. With Los Flamingos Golf and Country Club under construction, along with more hotels in the same area, the Costa del Sol will soon have even more high-quality courses to attract golfing visitors.

The Costa del Sol ends at Estepona before passing into the Sotogrande/Cádiz area, and we have divided the Andalucía golfing areas accordingly.

1 *Almerimar*

Almerimar Golf Club, Urb. Almerimar, 04700
El Ejido Almería, Andalucía
TEL: *950 49 74 54* **FAX:** *950 49 72 33*
EMAIL: *almerimar@golf-andalucia.net*
LOCATION: *Off the Motorway Almería–Málaga,*
towards El Ejido.
COURSE: *18 holes, 5981m/6541yd, par 72,*
SSS 72
GREEN FEES: *££££*
FACILITIES: *Clubhouse, driving range, buggy hire,*
hand trolley hire, pitching and putting greens, practice
bunker, golf tuition, club repair, club hire, caddy, pro-
shop, restaurant, bar, swimming pool, tennis court, horse
riding, hotel on site, apartments and showers.

This is a hospitable course for all levels of golfers, with spacious fairways and large, receptive greens. Problems occur if you are not accurate off the tees and stray off the well-defined, tree-lined fairways and into the variety of palms and thicker scrub.

The course presents a stiff opening par 5, a dogleg right where a well-positioned drive is essential to progress further along this tight, tree-lined corridor. A large bunker at the right turn will catch those that risk cutting the corner. A tight and lengthy par 4 at the 2nd (Stroke Index 1) will punish if the tee shot is not straight. The course then settles into a less arduous rhythm. Water comes into play on several holes, especially the 8th, 9th, 11th and 12th.

The course's overall short length, especially from the forward tees, is ideal for average players, but the great unknown factor here for every golfer is the wind. The trees offer some protection, but this can imbue a false sense of confidence.

The off-course amenities are good with a large, modern clubhouse and the Melia Golf Almerimar hotel on site.

Below: Almerimar has found favour with golfers seeking less crowded fairways. Generally the course is wide and accommodating, but the strong winds that are common to the area make the course that much more difficult.

2 La Envia

*La Envia Golf Club, Ctra. Alicún km 10, 300,
04738 Vícar. Almería, Andalucía*
TEL: *950 55 96 56* **FAX:** *950 55 96 42*
EMAIL: *envia@golf-andalucia.net*
LOCATION: *On the Motorway Puerto
Lumbreras-Adra, towards Málaga. 10km away
from Almería.*
COURSE: *18 holes, 5860m/6408yd, par 72,
SSS 70*
GREEN FEES: *££+*
FACILITIES: *Clubhouse, driving range, buggy
hire, hand and electric trolley hire, pitching and putting
greens, practice bunker, club repair, club hire, pro-shop,
restaurant, bar, swimming pool, tennis court and
showers.*

La Envia Golf Club is another example of a
fairly new development in an area that is
keen to cash in on the tourist bonanza
that has taken place further down the
coast. While development is prolific, most of
it is in good taste and the golf facilities at
courses such as La Envia are fundamental
to the area's success.

This course is set in a very picturesque
location with a mountainous backdrop.
These outcrops help to decrease the intense
winds that are a prominent feature of
this region.

La Envia's fairways are not as yet well
defined, with rather sparse vegetation and
little rough. However, there are still plenty
of challenges to face. Water comes into play
on the 3rd, 4th, 5th and 13th holes. The 9th
hole is a par 4 of 377m/412yd doglegging
left from the visitors' tee. This demands a
good, well-positioned drive to see and gain the
green in two. The 14th hole is a straight-ahead
par 4 but could pose problems if you have to
play into the wind.

Bunkering throughout the course
is most effective. Another determining factor
on La Envia is the greens, which are often
sloped or raised and not particularly easy to
hold. This is especially the case on the two
closing holes.

3 Playa Serena

*Playa Serena Golf Club, Autovía Málaga-Almería,
04740 Roquetas de Mar, Andalucía*
TEL: *950 33 30 55* **FAX:** *950 33 30 55*
EMAIL: *playaserena@golf-andalucia.net*
LOCATION: *N340 Málaga–Almería and
turn south towards Roquetas de Mar,
25km away.*
COURSE: *18 holes, 6070m/6638yd, par 72,
SSS 72*
GREEN FEES: *£££*
FACILITIES: *Clubhouse, driving range, buggy
hire, hand trolley hire, pitching and putting greens,
practice bunker, club hire, pro-shop, restaurant,
bar, swimming pool and showers.*

In concert with the development of this
area, Playa Serena gives a good option for
golfers wishing to enjoy a bit of variety.

Peter Allis and Angel Gallardo designed
this delightful little course. It consists of two
loops extending from the clubhouse, with
many water features presenting challenges
throughout. There is also the attraction of a
variety of exotic, migratory birds at particular
times of the year.

The course is only metres away from the
Mediterranean and is generally flat with
small, well-protected greens employing either
water or strategic bunkering. Wind is a
factor for most of the year. Combined with
the many water hazards, this can lead to
higher than anticipated scoring. Twelve holes
are affected by varying sizes of pools.
The rough is kept high and unforgiving,
partly to help define the flat terrain but
also adding to the challenge.

A good tee shot is essential on the 7th, a
longer than average par 5. Unless you can play
a sound draw, regulation is not easily
achieved due to the left dogleg. To lay-up
for position here will leave two solid
strokes to reach the green with out-of-bounds
down the length of the right side and
a psychologically trying prospect for
fairway woods.

Seve – Spanish Hero

More perhaps than any other golfer, Severiano Ballesteros has exerted a great influence on golf in Europe. This charming man, a true golfing wizard and consummate gentleman, dominated the game in Europe and the US from the mid-1970s to the late 1980s.

Seve's illustrious career started on the beaches of his home town of Pedrena on the north coast of Spain. Here young Seve would spend hours hitting pebbles with a rusty old 3-iron, developing his famous flexibility and shot-making ability. With a meteoric rise through the amateur ranks, Seve turned professional at 16. At 19 he grabbed the golfing world's imagination when he was the runner-up at the British Open Championship in 1976.

Above: Few golfers have done more to inspire than Seve Ballesteros.

The Spaniard's first major win came three years later with the Open at Royal Lytham, and the following year he donned the Master's green jacket at Augusta. 1983 saw a return to victory at Augusta. He won another Open championship at St Andrews in 1984 and a final Open at Lytham in 1988. As Ben Crenshaw said of Seve at the height of his powers, 'He plays shots I don't even see in my dreams'. With fellow countryman José María Olazábal he formed a dynamic, Hispanic double act that attracted followers the world over.

Since then, with a nagging back injury and a family of three, the drive that had once set him apart from others has perhaps diminished. But the public's admiration for the charismatic Spaniard continues. His appeal has transcended the game of golf and brought much pleasure to both golfers and non-golfers.

Seve's performance as European team captain during the 1997 Ryder Cup showed the genius and determination that he had applied to his own playing career. His abilities were transmitted to the team that he cajoled and implored to a dazzling performance. 'Seve seemed to be everywhere at once,' said his teammates as he hurled from one side of the course to the other offering support and advice.

The Seve Ballesteros Trophy

Although it is several years since he has played at the level he became famed for, there is always a feeling that Severiano Ballesteros is not yet finished. As captain of the new Ryder Cup-style match between the Continent of Europe versus Great Britain and Ireland, he led his European team to victory over Colin Montgomerie's squad. The inaugural match of 'The Seve Ballesteros Trophy' was played in Sunningdale, England in April 2000 when Seve beat all the odds to defeat world number three Colin Montgomerie in the opening singles match.

'This was a point that we felt was secure,' said Montgomerie after the match. 'We felt 85 per cent certain that I would win that game – and I didn't. Hopefully next time it will be different but you never know. When Seve is captain he seems impossible to beat.'

4 Anoreta

*Anoreta Golf Club Avda. De Golf s/n, 29730
Rincon de la Victoria, Málaga, Andalucía*
TEL: *952 40 40 00* **FAX:** *952 40 40 50*
EMAIL: *anoreta@golf-andalucia.net*
LOCATION: *12km from Málaga in El Rincon de la
Victoria.*
COURSE: *18 holes, 5673m/6204yd, Par 72,
SSS 70*
GREEN FEES: *££££*
FACILITIES: *Clubhouse, driving range, buggy hire,
hand and electric trolley hire, pitching and putting greens,
practice bunker, golf tuition, club repair, club hire, caddy,
pro-shop, restaurant, bar, swimming pool, changing room
and showers.*

The 'Costa del Golf', as it has become known, starts on the west side of Málaga with development east of the city relatively sparse. Anoreta Golf Club opened in 1990 as a nine-hole and extended four years later. It is now well worth an eastward excursion if you are not staying near here. Designed by Ryder Cup hero José María Canizares, it is built upon hilly terrain overlooking the Mediterranean and offers some tremendous views as well as a good golfing challenge.

The fairways tend to be generous, as do the greens, but it is the surfeit of wide, well-positioned water hazards that make their mark on a player's card. Water comes into play on no fewer than 11 holes, with the par 4 17th being the most memorable. A long stretch of water on the left leaves little landing area from the tee. This forces the inclination to play for safety, although the thought of a long iron into the green is equally daunting. This shot can easily find the sand or a second lake to the left and behind this green.

The coastal views from the 3rd hole are breathtaking, but from this high position it is also easy for the wind to take the ball. The crack of a good drive is most rewarding here as the hole drops around 25m/30yd to a wide fairway – but be conscious of breezes that tend to follow this embankment.

5 Guadalhorce

*Guadalhorce Golf Club, Ctra. Cartama km7,
Campanillas, 29590 Málaga, Andalucía*
TEL: *952 17 93 78* **FAX:** *952 17 93 72*
EMAIL: *guadalhorce@golf-andalucia.net*
LOCATION: *On the road towards Cartama, 7km from
Málaga Airport. Off the motorway, exit 238, Cartama.
Close to the centre of Málaga City.*
COURSE: *18 holes, 5860m/6409yd, par 72,
SSS 71*
GREEN FEES: *££+*
FACILITIES: *Clubhouse, driving range, covered driving
range, buggy hire, hand trolley hire, putting green,
practice bunker, club repair, club hire, pro-shop,
restaurant, bar, sauna and showers.*

Situated close to Málaga's busy urban sprawl, this course is an oasis of greenery and serenity. The imposing 18th-century manor house, now converted into a charming clubhouse, is surrounded by the course.

The front nine holes play over undulating parkland, by and large flat but swelling at points with a variety of scattered trees. The back nine, playing down towards the river, offers more variety with noticeable earthworks and lots of water. This is quite different in nature from the forerunning holes, and is more American in design.

Punitive rough is a characteristic of the opening holes, so work with long irons or fairway woods to avoid straying off the fairways and into trouble. Go for position to attack the greens, which are usually large and receptive. The holes are not long on the front half, so this is possible. The 4th is a birdie opportunity, a par 5 at only 441m/482yd, but be sure to go for the pin on this elongated green – three putts are common. There are two double greens here (an unusual feature in this part of the world), at the 6th and 8th and the 12th and 16th. These must be approached with the pin in mind rather than leave lengthy putts. The back nine is enjoyable off the elevated tees as there is more room and less chance of losing the ball to snarling rough.

6 Parador Málaga

Parador Málaga del Golf Club, Apartado 324, 29080
Málaga, Andalucía
Tel: 952 38 12 55 **Fax:** 952 38 21 41
Location: From the N340 turn off for Cotin-
Churriana.
Course: 18 holes, 6204m/6785yd, par 72,
SSS 72
Green Fees: ££
Facilities: Clubhouse, driving range, buggy hire,
hand trolley hire, pitching and putting greens, practice
bunker, golf tuition, club repair, club hire, caddy, pro-
shop, restaurant, bar, swimming pool, tennis court, hotel
on site, apartments and showers.

PARADOR MALAGA

HOLE	YD	M	PAR	HOLE	YD	M	PAR
1	489	447	5	10	311	284	4
2	368	337	4	11	214	196	3
3	311	284	4	12	543	497	5
4	453	414	4	13	180	165	3
5	417	381	4	14	470	430	4
6	190	174	3	15	419	383	4
7	388	355	4	16	489	447	5
8	530	485	5	17	365	334	4
9	203	186	3	18	443	405	4
OUT	3350	3063	36	IN	3435	3141	36

6785YD • 6204M • PAR 72

Many traditionalists will name this as one of their favourite courses in Spain, and indeed Europe. It is an example of how golf courses were designed in the heyday of golf architecture through the 1920s and 30s. It therefore stands out as a 'classic' layout in an area that is dominated by contemporary, American golf design.

While the course does not compare to a true links in the 'Scottish' sense, the tight turf, sandy subsoil and fresh breezes blowing along the Málaga seashore make it a good approximation. Built in 1929 by the Scottish architect Tom Simpson, who also worked on Scotland's famous Turnberry and Muirfield courses, the course and the *Parador* (hotel) that it surrounds are redolent of tradition and good taste. The entire complex comes highly recommended and should be experienced.

The course is an excellent test of golf and many major tournaments have been staged here. The first Amateur Cup was held here as well as the European Tour 'Tourespania', and the Andalucian Masters

Open came here in 1992 and again in 1999. Spanish golf star Miguel Angel Jímenez did much of his ground work here while employed as a caddy.

While it has an impressive pedigree, the course is quite easy for high handicappers as it is flat with a wonderful sandy loam and thin rough. Its seaside conditions are most evident from the 7th through to the 12th, with these holes open to the nearby beach. The course is often windy and this can be a considerable factor in play. The rest of the course presents tree-lined avenues with greens surrounded by a variety of pine and flowering bushes.

The best challenge occurs at the 7th, a long hole (especially into the wind) at 355m/388yd

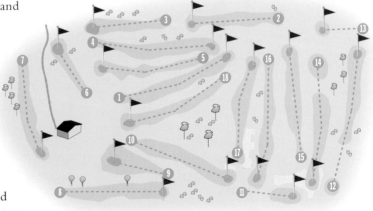

considering the narrow design of the fairway with fenced out of bounds on the right and the *Parador* to the left. A driver could be judged risky off the tee especially if you do not wish to risk the embarrassment of hooking into the hotel. The 12th, a par 5, presents a narrow opening off the tee and ends with a tricky, elevated green. From here, the course takes on more dramatic swells and dips, the links-like characteristics more pronounced, especially in front of the greens. The 14th is similarly undulating with a blind tee shot over a rising swell into a long and tight fairway lined with trees. This is an average par 5 with water left and right. It is best played as a bogie, especially considering the water around the green. The 18th is a par 4, long at 405m/443yd with a

Above: The view from the Parador balcony! Spanish golf star Miguel Angel Jímenez worked here as a caddy.

dogleg right and, like many of the holes, undulating especially nearer the green. These are the holes that will give problems to any level of golfer.

Right: Parador Málaga is a links course playing into pine woods, before opening out on to more flat, open links land and the subsequent coastal winds.

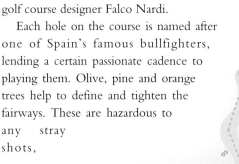 *Lauro*

*Lauro Golf Club, Los Caracolillos s/n 29130 Alhaurín
de la Torre, Andalucía*
Tel: *952 41 27 67* **Fax:** *952 41 47 57*
Email: *lauro@golf-andalucia.net*
Location: *Off the road C344, km77. Between
Alhaurín de la Torre and Alhaurín el Grande.*
Course: *18 holes, 5977m/6536yd, par 72, SSS 70*
Green Fees: *££+*
Facilities: *Clubhouse, driving range, buggy hire,
hand trolley hire, pitching and putting greens, practice
bunker, club hire, pro-shop, restaurant, tennis court,
horse riding and showers.*

Lauro Golf Club nestles inside a stunning locale and covers an apparently unspoilt natural terrain. The course is around 330 metres above sea level and plays around a 200-year-old converted farmhouse. This serves as a most pleasant clubhouse with a shaded courtyard now converted into a splendid outdoor restaurant. Opened in 1992, it was the last project of the celebrated Italian golf course designer Falco Nardi.

Each hole on the course is named after one of Spain's famous bullfighters, lending a certain passionate cadence to playing them. Olive, pine and orange trees help to define and tighten the fairways. These are hazardous to any stray shots,

*Above: The views and immediate terrain of Lauro Golf
Club are inspiring.*

threatening the driving proposition considerably. The 4th is an unusual par 3 of only 155m/170yd, but clubbing is difficult to judge. The water hazards of the 9th and 18th can alternatively threaten the drive and approach shots calling for careful consideration.

8 *Torrequebrada*

*Torrequebrada Golf Club, N340 km220, 29630
Benalmádena, Málaga, Andalucía* **TEL:** *952 44 27 42*
FAX: *952 56 11 29*
EMAIL: *torrequebrada@golf-andalucia.net*
LOCATION: *On the road N340, 220km, towards the
development Torrequebrada.*
COURSE: *18 holes, 5513m/6029yd, par 72, SSS 70*
GREEN FEES: *££££+*
FACILITIES: *Clubhouse, driving range, buggy hire,
hand trolley hire, pitching and putting greens, practice
bunker, club repair, club hire, pro-shop, restaurant, bar,
swimming pool, tennis court, sauna and showers.*

Pepe Gancedo gained a great reputation as a course designer in Spain, mainly due to his ability to blend a golf course into its existing terrain without too much earth moving. This has led, in certain areas, to some rather pronounced golfing situations. Anyone who loves to play golf within a natural setting combined with wonderful vistas will appreciate Gancedo's efforts.

Torrequebrada is one of the more favoured courses in this busy tourist area stretching between Benalmádena and Fuengirola. It has been established since the mid-1970s and so has a maturity not always evident on the Costa's many newer golfing venues. The generous fairways are solidly lined with palms

*Above: Torrequebrada is one of the more favoured courses
on the Costa del Sol.*

and pines, not presenting too much difficulty unless seriously wayward, but beyond them the ball will probably be lost. While lost balls cost points to the 'wild driver', it is the fast and fiery raised greens, patrolled by drying winds, which add the strokes to a good players' card.

Throughout this undulating course (which is best tackled with a cart), there is a tremendous variety of situations making all sorts of demands on a player's abilities. With multiple levels and sloping greens, each shot must be considered.

The 16th is the most memorable hole. Here the drive on this dogleg right must carry water to a safe landing zone before crossing a second lake on to the elevated green. The 7th plays down towards the sea with a lovely backdrop and, as a par 4, can be driven with a following wind.

The clubhouse is particularly welcoming and it is a pleasure to sit on the upstairs balcony after a round and enjoy the views of the 18th with a cooling breeze off the Mediterranean. Visitors are welcome to use the clubhouse swimming pool and its other amenities.

 Mijas

Mijas Golf Club, Los Olivos and Los Lagos Courses
Ctra. de Coin, km3, 29640 Fuengirola, Andalucía
TEL: *952 47 68 43* **FAX:** *952 46 79 43*
EMAIL: *mijas@golf-andalucia.net*
LOCATION: *Road N340 Málaga-Cádiz. Take the*
road towards Coin, 3km.
COURSE: *Los Olivos Course: 18 holes,*
5545m/6064yd, par 72, SSS 70 **Los Lagos Course:**
18 holes, 5975m/6534yd, par 71, SSS 72
GREEN FEES: *£££*
FACILITIES: *Clubhouse, driving range, buggy hire,*
hand and electric trolley hire, pitching and putting greens,
practice bunker, club repair, club hire, pro-shop,
restaurant, bar and showers.

The Mijas complex (consisting of two courses, Los Olivos and Los Lagos) is the most popular golfing resort certainly in the area and most likely in Spain. Both courses are relatively flat and not overly difficult for mid to high handicappers. The complex is also well organised and holds frequent 'open' competitions that help attract golf tourists.

The Los Olivos course is the newer, designed by Robert Trent Jones. It features less water than its neighbour. It employs the vagaries of terrain to good effect and demands

Above: Mijas presents one of the most popular venues for
package holiday golfers.

stricter attention to accuracy off the tees, the fairways being narrower. Trees and an undulating progress make it strategically more interesting. The greens are also smaller and often elevated. All this adds up to a very different test from Los Lagos.

The more favoured course, Los Lagos, offers wide fairways, large raised greens, frequent and gaping bunkers as well as many water hazards. There is good opportunity on many holes to let loose with the driver, but this is balanced by American-style target golf into the greens. The judicious placement of bunkers helps to strengthen the course. There are eight lakes in all and the course is generally flatter so is easy on the legs.

If you want to play both courses in a day, consider walking the Los Lagos in the morning and hiring a buggy for the second Los Olivos round. To reach the Mijas complex follow the MA425 or you will end up in Mijas village. This is a worthwhile excursion, but not if you have tee times booked.

10 *Alhaurín*

Alhaurín Golf and Hotel Resort, Ctra. de Mijas, Alhaurín el Grande, Andalucía
TEL: *952 59 58 00* **FAX:** *952 59 60 50*
EMAIL: *alhaurin@golf-andalucia.net*
LOCATION: *From Fuengirola take the MA409, towards Mijas.*
COURSE: *18 holes, 6221m/6803yd, par 72, SSS 74*
GREEN FEES: *£££*
FACILITIES: *Clubhouse, driving range, buggy hire, hand and electric trolley hire, golf tuition, club hire, pro-shop, restaurant, bar, swimming pool, tennis court, horse riding, sauna and showers. 9-hole, par 3 course, 18-hole par 3 course for youngsters plus adjoining 4-star hotel with tennis, swimming pool and horse riding.*

Alhaurín is a relatively new course set in the green folds of the Sierra de Mijas. Designed by Severiano Ballesteros, this new complex is about 15km (9 miles) from the coast and a dizzying 340m/372yd above sea level.

The course can be criticised for unfairness because of the recurring and often acute tilts to the fairways that will carry a well-placed tee shot into trouble. A faded tee shot will often serve best here.

The mountain landscape makes up to some degree for any such problems along with beautiful man-made lakes and an attractive terraced quality to many of the holes. The course is still under development, with minor adjustments being made to provide for higher handicaps such as reducing the rough and pushing out of bounds back to allow more room for error.

The course's most challenging holes are found on the back nine. Ballesteros shows his flair for design particularly at the 18th, a par 4. It is recommended that a buggy is hired as the ups and downs of the course make it almost impossible to play without one.

Below: Alhaurín's rugged landscape calls for careful placement of the ball.

11 *La Cala*

La Cala Golf Club, North Course and South Course
La Cala de Mijas, 229647 Mijas Costa, Andalucía
TEL: *952 66 90 00* **FAX:** *952 66 90 34*
EMAIL: *cala@golf-andalucia.net*
LOCATION: *N340 Málaga-Cádiz, towards Fuengirola
until you get to la Cala del Moral.*
COURSE: *South Course: 18 holes, 5960m/6518yd,
par 71, SSS 71* **North Course:** *18 holes,
5723m/6259yd, par 73, SSS 72*
GREEN FEES: *£££+*
FACILITIES: *Clubhouse, driving range, buggy hire,
hand and electric trolley hire, pitching and putting greens,
practice bunker, golf tuition, club repair, club hire, pro-
shop, restaurant, bar, swimming pool, tennis court,
fitness centre, sauna and showers.*

L a Cala is the winter headquarters of the
Swedish Golf Federation. It is an 'up-hill,
down-dale' layout of two 18-holes designed
by American architect Cabell B. Robinson. It
has a David Leadbetter Golf Academy and a
six-hole, par 3 course. A buggy is highly
recommended to reach the high points.

There is little between these two courses for
the good player off the back tees, but high
handicappers might find the South Course a
little too trying. Both courses necessitate shot-
making skills to reach and hold the often-
elevated greens. The North Course is generally
considered the better of the two. It presents
soaring prospects from many tees. This
becomes apparent at the par 5 15th, with its
grand outlook over the South Course towards
the sea. From such a height wind can be
influential. Even at the short 16th, which plays
over a small kidney-shaped pond to a mid-
sized green, what appears an easy proposition
can work out otherwise. Although the North
Course was designed for competition with
some long par 4s and challenging par 3s, the
wide fairways and variable tee positions make it
acceptable for high handicappers. Water is not
a major feature, but there are plenty of
cavernous sand traps.

The South Course is an undulating,
climbing course playing to elevated greens
with slopes that can easily carry a ball away.
There is generally adequate room off the tees,
but the rough can be punishing.

*Below: The par 3 16th on the North Course is short
but testing.*

12 *Santa María*

Santa María Golf and Country Club N340 km192,
Urb. Elviría, 29600 Marbella, Andalucía
TEL: *952 83 03 86/8* **FAX:** *952 83 08 70*
EMAIL: *santamaria@golf-andalucia.net*
LOCATION: *15km east of Marbella off the N340.*
COURSE: *18 holes, 5352m/5853yd, par 70,*
SSS 70
GREEN FEES: *£££*
FACILITIES: *Clubhouse, driving range, covered driving range, buggy hire, hand trolley hire, pitching and putting greens, practice bunker, golf tuition, club repair, club hire, caddy, pro-shop, restaurant, bar, fitness centre, sauna and showers.*

Above: Santa María course offers some exciting prospects as it climbs and then descends back to the clubhouse. The use of this varied terrain is admirable.

Occasionally on the Costa del Sol, a gem appears that you might not have heard of before. Santa María is a delightful course that has become increasingly popular since its development from a nine-hole to an 18-hole course. The club staged the Andalucian PGA Tournament in 1997.

The course is built within two separate valleys. The cart paths and course climb through a short but tricky arrangement before turning to descend back towards the clubhouse. A buggy is recommended to cope with the climbs.

There are four wide lakes with a good example at the 9th hole, which is easy enough to carry. This, combined with a variety of natural vegetation, forms the main hazard. Some would say that the varying level of the terrain also adds to the challenge.

The 7th is perhaps the most beautiful hole on this pleasant layout, with a green that is well defended by sand traps. The 11th is also a feature hole with a lake and waterfall bordering the green. On the back nine from elevated tees the greens are generous, but can make for long putts.

Visitors are welcome to play in the regular weekly competitions, which are usually held on Wednesdays and Sundays.

13 Marbella

Marbella Golf Club, N340, km188, 29600 Marbella, Andalucía
TEL: *952 83 05 00* **FAX:** *952 83 53 43*
EMAIL: *marbellagolf@golf-andalucia.net*
LOCATION: *Road N340 Málaga-Cádiz. Pass Las Chapas, deflection to the right. In front of la Playa de los Monteros and la Playa de Alicante.*
COURSE: *18 holes, 5558m/6078yd, par 71, SSS 71*
GREEN FEES: *££££*
FACILITIES: *Clubhouse, driving range, buggy hire, hand trolley hire, pitching and putting greens, practice bunker, club repair, club hire, pro-shop, restaurant, bar, fitness centre, sauna, Jacuzzi and showers.*

Marbella is a classy club set between the N340 and the new *autopista*. The clubhouse is large and elegant with a wonderful outdoor terrace overlooking the 18th. The course is not dissimilar to its near neighbour, Santa María, playing over the same type of stepped terrain. The fairways appear to be melted onto the surrounding rolling landscape.

While the course is definitely American in its character – it was designed by Robert Trent Jones – the natural vegetation has been left in good order and comprises a major defence of this course.

Large bunkers protect generous, sometimes raised, greens, and water comes into play on four occasions. The fairways sweep left and right – in fact it appears that half of the holes are dogleg right while the others are dogleg left. This forces the golfer to use a variety of shots. The course is therefore a good test for low handicappers who have the flexibility to play these situations.

There is not an easy portion to any part of this course. The par 3s require pinpoint precision, while the par 5s are true and difficult to reach in two. The 17th is a fine example, a drive uphill leaving another sound fairway wood before attacking the green. The consistent and demanding character of the holes means that you will not get away with anything here. The course favours golfers who can provide both length and accuracy.

Below: A welcome beer on the balcony follows Marbella's final hole.

14 *Rio Real*

Rio Real Golf Club, N340 km185, Marbella, Andalucía
TEL: *952 77 95 09* **FAX:** *952 77 21 40*
EMAIL: *rioreal@golf-andalucia.net*
LOCATION: *On the east side of Marbella, turn in front of Playa de los Monteros.*
COURSE: *18 holes, 5886m/6437yd, par 72, SSS 71*
GREEN FEES: *£££*
FACILITIES: *Clubhouse, driving range, buggy hire, hand trolley hire, pitching and putting greens, practice bunker, club repair, club hire, pro-shop, restaurant, bar, swimming pool and showers.*

This is a luxurious-looking layout as apparent from the shaded clubhouse with avenues of rich green fairways playing through tall, mature palms. Being almost at sea level, the course curves gently towards the beach before turning back to the clubhouse.

As one of the Costa del Sol's oldest courses built close to the town of Marbella, Rio Real demands a certain respect, although it is not a particularly tough test.

The palm trees give excellent shelter from the sun through the warmer months and yet, while they will deflect a badly struck ball, they do not hamper speed of play. The River Real intersects the course at various points, coming into play for the unwary golfer. The 4th and 5th holes are reached via an underpass and then open out to the sea.

Playing golf at Rio Real is all about enjoyment, and most people will find that the

Above: Rio Real comes near to the sea but mostly consists of tree-lined parkland.

setting for this fine course certainly facilitates an enjoyable round.

15 *La Dama de Noche*

La Dama de Noche Golf Club, Apartado 79, 29600 Marbella, Andalucía
TEL: *952 81 81 50* **FAX:** *952 81 70 06*
EMAIL: *damanoche@golf-andalucia.net*
LOCATION: *Situated in el Camino del Angel, Rio Verde just east of Puerto Banus.*
COURSE: *9 holes, 2728m/2983yd, par 36, SSS 72*
GREEN FEES: *££+*
FACILITIES: *Clubhouse, buggy hire, hand trolley hire, putting green, club hire, caddy, pro-shop, restaurant and bar.*

La Dama de Noche Golf Club is Marbella's only floodlit golf course and is thriving, though there have been some wrangles caused by its bright lights being so close to the N340 coastal road. It is set next to the glamorous satellite town of Puerto Banus. Although only nine holes, there is something novel about playing golf after dark and the course can be quite busy at times.

La Dama de Noche purports to be a 24-hour facility, but there are restrictions. Bookings should be made in advance and a set number of players booked to use the course before it will open in the evening.

It's a short course and good fun for a group out for a relaxing bit of frivolity. In the daytime it is a good outing for novice golfers with little or no rough. 'La Dama de Noche', as well as meaning 'the lady of the night', is the name of a plant with a nocturnal fragrance that is commonly reputed to keep mosquitoes at bay. However, it would be wise to take along a can of insect repellent just in case.

16 *Aloha*

Aloha Golf Club, Urb. Aloha, Nueva Andalucía,
29660 Marbella, Andalucía
TEL: *952 81 37 50* **FAX:** *952 81 23 89*
EMAIL: *aloha@golf-andalucia.net*
LOCATION: *Málaga–Cádiz road, 180km, in front of*
Puerto Banus. In the complex Aloha, in Nueva
Andalucía.
COURSE: *18 holes, 5936m/6492yd, par 72, SSS 72*
GREEN FEES: *££££££*
FACILITIES: *Clubhouse, driving range, buggy hire,*
hand and electric trolley hire, pitching and putting greens,
practice bunker, club repair, club hire, pro-shop,
restaurant, bar, swimming pool, tennis court, sauna and
showers.

This was one of the first courses in the famous 'Valley of Golf', a wealthy urban spur to Marbella and Puerto Banus. The course has required some upgrading in recent years but this has now been completed.

Set on the valley floor, it provides easy walking but is not entirely flat. There are some surprising dips and rises with many elevated tees and greens. Occasional water and a variety of mature plantations also feature and can tighten many holes considerably. Play demands straight hitting off the tees, but this is rewarded with a good set-up position into the greens. Most of the challenge comes on the large and subtly undulating putting surfaces, where it is not easy to read the line or judge the pace.

This is a private club where members have priority, but it remains welcoming and is well worth investigating.

17 *Las Brisas*

Real Club Las Brisas, Ctra. Málaga–Cádiz, km174,
29660 Nueva Andalucía, Andalucía
TEL: *952 81 08 75* **FAX:** *952 81 55 18*
EMAIL: *brisas@golf-andalucia.net*
LOCATION: *Marbella's 'Valley of Golf' behind Puerto*
Banus and signposted, although this can be confusing.
COURSE: *18 holes, 5893m/6445yd, par 72,*
SSS 72
GREEN FEES: *££££££+*
FACILITIES: *Clubhouse, driving range, covered driving*
range, buggy hire, hand and electric trolley hire, pitching
and putting greens, practice bunker, club repair, club hire,
caddy, pro-shop, restaurant, bar and sauna.

This Robert Trent Jones design is an example of a pristine, perfectly-maintained golf course. The ambience is more Sunningdale than Costa del Sol and if you are willing to pay the elevated green fees and manage to book a tee time you will enjoy this.

The terrain is rolling, with mountainous views off to the northeast. Proficient driving is required but it is not a prerequisite for a good score. It is the well-judged placement of sand and water that calls for confident approach strikes, especially into the often-raised greens. There are 10 stretches of water on the course, affecting a dozen of the holes.

The back nine is characterised by a variety of close-planted trees. Each of these holes sweeps left or right in a balanced rhythm through avenues and out into open, water-guarded expanses. The need for accuracy prevails and you may use just about every club in the bag.

Above: Aloha, one of the first courses to be created in the 'Valley of Golf' to the north of Puerto Banus.

18 Los Naranjos

Los Naranjos Golf Club, Nueva Andalucía, 29960,
Marbella, Andalucía
Tel: 952 81 24 28 **Fax:** 952 81 14 28
Email: naranjosgolf@golf-andalucia.net
Location: Off the road N340 Málaga–Cádiz,
174km. Pass Marbella, towards Puerto Banus, follow
signs.
Course: 18 holes, 6038m/6603yd, par 72, SSS 72
Green Fees: ££££
Facilities: Clubhouse, driving range, covered driving
area, buggy hire, hand and electric trolley hire, pitching
and putting greens, practice bunker, club repair, club hire,
pro-shop, restaurant, bar, fitness centre, sauna and
showers.

Los Naranjos provides a good workout for players with a long game, with long spectacular drives down into valleys and uphill approach shots to greens surrounded by giant multiple bunkers.

There is a marked difference between the two halves of this course, leading one to wonder whether this has been a universal objective of southern Spain's course designers or just a recurring quirk of the land. The first half of Los Naranjos plunges from the tee and rises again to the green. Lengths are reasonable and opportunities arise if you can fly the elaborate bunkering. Otherwise, playing out of sand to a raised green can be especially difficult.

The back nine has less exaggerated movement, verging on being flat until the 18th. There are testing short holes on this course, of which the 12th is a good example. To compensate, the 14th is a massive par 5 of 500m/547yd.

The course gradually climbs to finish with one of the best par 4s in Spain. The 18th needs a powerful drive to give the optimum attacking position across water to the raised green. The flag position is difficult to judge and so pay careful attention to the distance markers.

Los Naranjos' clubhouse is very welcoming and its restaurant serves excellent food.

Below: Los Naranjos' 18th is one of the best finishing holes in Spain.

19 *La Quinta*

La Quinta Golf Club, Ctra. Ronda, km3.5, 29660, Nueva Andalucía, Andalucía
TEL: *952 78 34 62* **FAX:** *952 78 34 66*
EMAIL: *laquinta@golf-andalucia.net*
LOCATION: *Continue through the 'Valley of Golf' behind Puerto Banus.*
COURSE: *18 holes, 5517m/6033yd, par 72, SSS 71*
GREEN FEES: *££££*
FACILITIES: *Clubhouse, driving range, covered driving range, buggy hire, hand and electric trolley hire, pitching and putting greens, practice bunker, golf tuition centre, club hire, pro-shop, restaurant, bar, fitness centre, sauna and showers.*

Further up the valley from Los Naranjos, the terrain at La Quinta is more provoking and testing.

The fairways are generous enough but beware of trees, traps and water that come into play more than might be assumed from the elevated tees. Bunkering increases in its ferocity closer into the greens and one can easily watch a score escalate on what would first appear to be an easy hole.

The use of a 3-iron off the tees with consideration for placement of the next shot will yield a better score and a more enjoyable round.

It is safe to say that, in spite of some recent modifications, La Quinta's course is the preserve of the more experienced golfer. Meanwhile, the course's teaching academy is the obvious place to go for any players who want to learn the basics or to polish up their rusty skills.

20 *Guadalmina*

Guadalmina Golf Club, Urb. Guadalmina Alta, 29678 San Pedro de Alcantara, Andalucía
TEL: *952 88 34 55* **FAX:** *952 88 34 83*
EMAIL: *guadalmina@golf-andalucia.net*
LOCATION: *From Marbella, just beyond the Marbella Arch towards Estepona.*
COURSE: *North Course – 18 holes, 5874m/6424yd, par 70, SSS 70 South Course – 18 holes, 6025m/6589yd, par 72, SSS 71*
GREEN FEES: *£££*
FACILITIES: *Clubhouse, driving range, covered driving range, buggy hire, hand and electric trolley hire, pitching and putting greens, practice bunker, golf tuition, club repair, pro-shop, restaurant, bar and showers.*

Both the North and South courses are quite affable. The South Course is slightly longer and plays down to the beach next to the Golf Hotel Guadalmina. The best hole on the South Course is its longest, the 6th called Tipperary – a name Henry Cotton coined as it was such a long way. The 10th comes out of the trees at the Golf Hotel Guadalmina, leaving a refreshing view of beach and water with the flag dead ahead. The contrast from parkland to seaside links is marked, especially with a welcome seaside breeze. But the hole that everyone seems to remember is the par 3 11th. Depending on the wind, this hole can call for a pitch one day and a 6-iron the next.

The North Course is flatter and easier. Being the younger of the two it has lent itself to housing development, which encroaches in places. The clubhouse is rather dated but has its own sort of charm.

Above: Guadalmina South plays down to the beach.

21 *Los Arqueros*

*Los Arqueros Golf Club, Ctra. San Pedro de Alcántara,
Ronda 29670, Benahavis, Andalucía*
TEL: *952 78 81 32* **FAX:** *952 78 81 30*
EMAIL: *arqueros@golf-adalucia.net*
LOCATION: *From the N340, take the C339 towards
Ronda and club signposted to the left.*
COURSE: *18 holes, 5520m/6037yd, par 72,
SSS 72*
GREEN FEES: *£££*
FACILITIES: *Clubhouse, driving range, buggy hire,
hand trolley hire, pitching and putting greens, practice
bunker, club repair, club hire, caddy, pro-shop,
restaurant, bar and showers.*

*Above: Los Arqueros' steep banking will limit housing
development and leave the views unspoilt. Meanwhile,
the fairways and greens are sumptuous!*

There are areas of the Costa del Sol that are ripe for development and villas and apartments creep further inland from the coast. Inevitably a golf course is built to help attract buyers, and sometimes the construction is a little too confining.

However, set in a wide, green valley a few kilometres back from the coast, Los Arqueros Golf and Country Club looks most inviting from its approach road. Designed by Severiano Ballesteros, this is another course that is good for mid to high handicaps. It is not too long but starts off high at the 1st and 10th and descends to the valley floor for fairly level play. It does ascend at several holes such as the 8th, 9th and 18th again, so carts are advisable if you do not wish to overexert yourself.

There are some target holes where lack of precision can lose balls, but generally the course is not difficult and its lovely settings make it most enjoyable. 'Risk and reward' is the order of the day if you are out to score. Because of the steep banks housing is and will continue to be limited here.

22 Monte Mayor

Monte Mayor Golf Club, Urb. Los Naranjos Country
Club, Nueva Andalucía, 29660, Málaga.
TEL: 952 11 30 88 **FAX:** 952 11 30 87
EMAIL: montemayor@golf-andalucia.net
LOCATION: On the N340, look for the village of
Cancelada and follow signs for 8km. It is a wild, twisting
road to get there but persevere and you will be rewarded.
COURSE: 18 holes, 5354m/5855yd, par 71,
SSS 71
GREEN FEES: £££ including buggy
FACILITIES: Club hire, pro-shop, restaurant and bar.

It is an entertaining journey up to Monte
Mayor's mountain retreat. Signs are placed
along the winding, climbing track to
keep you going such as 'Nearly there!'
and 'Congratulations, You Made It!'
Compensation exists in the views down the
coast to Gibraltar. The final downhill
approach gives you a glimpse of the course,
which is exciting enough but the greatest
excitement comes when you are actually
playing it.

Monte Mayor is a course you will either
absolutely fall in love with and return again and

Below: Monte Mayor's mountain retreat.

again, or deeply loathe. Unless you are in total
control of your irons you will lose balls. There
is no room for error and it is not uncommon
to hear some choice expletive echo through
the hills. It is a spectacular course for those that
love a challenge and a nightmare for those that
need an airport runway to land a drive.

The layout climbs all the way up the Lomas
de Retamar valley roughly following a small
river bed. The setting is spectacular and the
small greens and fairway grass are always in
excellent condition. Carts are compulsory
following a one-way path that climbs all the
way up to the 9th then back down again.

This course can be most rewarding to those
that can play for position with irons. There are
only around three occasions where a wood is
required and rarely a driver at that. This can
prove very frustrating and costly to players
determined to squeeze out an extra few yards.

The course's best features are its serenity, its
stunning outlooks and its peacefulness – you
rarely see another group. There are no facilities
out on the course and so it is acceptable to take
a small picnic to enjoy around the 12th tee, the
course's highest point, allowing other groups to
play through.

23 Atalaya

*Atalaya Country Club, Ctra. Benahavis km0.7,
29688 Estepona, Andalucía*
TEL: *952 88 28 12* **FAX:** *952 88 78 97*
EMAIL: *atalaya@golf-andalucia.net*
LOCATION: *Take the road to Benahavis.*
COURSES: *Old Course: 18 holes, 5905m/6457yd,
par 72, SSS 72 New Course: 18 holes,
5082m/5558yd, par 72, SSS 67*
GREEN FEES: *£££*
FACILITIES: *Clubhouse, driving range, buggy hire,
hand trolley hire, pitching and putting greens, practice
bunker, golf tuition, club repair, pro-shop, restaurant,
bar and showers.*

Atalaya Old starts out well but is slightly disappointing in its general character. It is fairly flat and long with wide fairways so most of the challenge is in achieving distance. The best hole is undoubtedly the 7th, a par 3 with a large bunker on either side of the raised green and water in front. The par 4 3rd is long with heavy bunkering around 200m/219yd out as well as bunkers around the raised green.

It is a very long walk from the clubhouse to the 1st tee on the New, but no one should be walking this course unless they are a fell-runner or mountaineer. The New course opened in 1992 and is shorter and tighter. In many ways it is easier than its level elder neighbour despite being a lot hillier. It is a course to lay-up off the tee and put the emphasis on the approach shots for best results. For better players, the hole to stand out is the 18th, a long par 5 of 536m/586yd.

24 El Paraíso

*El Paraíso Golf Club, Ctra. de Cádiz km167, 29680
Estepona, Andalucía*
TEL: *952 88 38 46* **FAX:** *952 88 58 27*
EMAIL: *paraiso@golf-andalucia.net*
LOCATION: *Take the N340 for 14km from Marbella
and course entrance is off to the right.*
COURSE: *18 holes, 5729m/6265yd, par 71,
SSS 71*
GREEN FEES: *£££*
FACILITIES: *Clubhouse, driving range, buggy hire,
hand trolley hire, pitching and putting greens, practice
bunker, golf tuition, club hire, pro-shop, restaurant,
bar and showers.*

This is one of the oldest layouts on the coast, with the great Gary Player having a hand in designing it. The course occupies a valley floor so it is not too difficult to negotiate, with only a gentle roll to most fairways. The predominant vegetation is palms of varying sizes, but there is an abundance of flora including oleander, mimosas and jacaranda, making for a pleasant and yet not punishing environment.

There are lakes at the 7th and 13th but these do not present great difficulties. The 6th, a par 5, presents the stiffest test, a dogleg left with well-positioned bunkers off the tee and a second shot that is best placed left to avoid the lake. The green is distinctly tiered, calling for an accurate shot to roll up to the flag.

The clubhouse offers a pleasant and comfortable setting in which to relax after your game, especially sitting outside in the courtyard bistro.

*Above: Atalaya offers a varied challenge with its Old and
New courses, the New being fairly hilly while the Old is an
easier walking proposition.*

25 *Estepona*

*Estepona Golf Club, Ctra. N340, km150, 29680
Estepona, Andalucía*
TEL: *952 11 30 81* FAX: *952 11 30 80*
WWW: *www.esteponagolf.com*
EMAIL: *rory.leader@esteponagolf.com*
LOCATION: *On the N340 on the west side of
Estepona.*
COURSE: *18 holes, 5610m/6135yd, par 72,
SSS 72*
GREEN FEES: *££*
FACILITIES: *Clubhouse, driving range, buggy hire,
hand trolley hire, putting green, club hire, pro-shop,
restaurant, bar and showers.*

The Estepona area has been a slower
development on the Costa del Sol and
Estepona Golf Club makes a rather refreshing
change from the other courses around
Marbella. There is less pressure here and,
although the course has been much improved
recently, there is still a rustic, natural
atmosphere that helps you to relax and enjoy
the round.

The undulating terrain follows a relatively
short routing that includes the aptly named 'Ski
Run', a long 3rd hole plunging back down to
road level. This is an easy proposition if you
strike a good drive and the resulting lie is
not awkward. If you are playing from
an uneven lie
many of the holes
require critical club
selection. At the
10th there are four
lakes to negotiate
and three bunkers
guard the green. In
general, Estepona
is a hilly course
and a buggy will
make your round
more comfortable.

The clubhouse
serves good quality
evening meals.

26 *La Duquesa*

*La Duquesa Golf and Country Club, N340 km145,
Manilva, Andalucía*
TEL: *952 89 07 25* FAX: *952 89 04 25*
EMAIL: *duquesa@golf-andalucia.net*
LOCATION: *On the N340, by La Duquesa just
beyond Manilva.*
COURSE: *18 holes, 5672m/6203yd, par 72,
SSS 70*
GREEN FEES: *££*
FACILITIES: *Clubhouse, driving range, covered driving
range, buggy hire, hand trolley hire, pitching and putting
greens, practice bunker, golf tuition, club repair, club hire,
pro-shop, restaurant, bar, swimming pool, tennis courts,
squash, fitness centre, sauna, jacuzzi and showers.*

La Duquesa is designed around a hill that
overlooks the Mediterranean, the Rock
of Gibraltar and, on a clear day, the north
coast of Africa. The back nine here could
benefit from the use of a buggy but generally
it is not impossible to walk this course. It is
not an overly demanding tract and has gently
undulating greens so the average golfer will
find it flattering. When the trouble does come
it is usually in the form of bunkering or for
wild shots, rough.

Play gently here and the course could yield
a fine score. The 7th is a birdie opportunity, as
are the other par 5s on the course, but place
the ball at the
dogleg corner
rather than try to
cut it. Mistakes are
the only way you
will blot the score
card. The 17th
hole is a dynamic
par 3, compact but
cunning if the
frequent westerly
wind seizes the
ball. There is only
a spattering of
water to encounter
on the course.

*Above: La Duquesa will yield to a relaxed approach,
especially on the back nine where the terrain becomes
more hilly.*

REGIONAL DIRECTORY

Where to stay

At the eastern end of the Costa del Sol, the four-star **Hotel Parador Málaga del Golf** (952 38 12 55) is highly recommended. It's classy, relaxed, close to the action in Málaga and Torremolinos and is surrounded by one of the best golf courses in the region. Special discounted green fees are available to Parador guests. In Málaga itself the **Parador Gibralfaro** (952 22 19 02) is good though small and the views over the coast are sensational. The five-star **Hotel Byblos** (952 24 73 05) looks directly over the two Mijas courses. The five-star **La Cala Resort** (952 66 90 00) is yet another resort that offers golf on the doorstep. You pay for the privilege in the five-stars but bear in mind that there are also lots of villas, apartments and hotel rooms that you can hire independently and at keener prices. The **Golf Hotel Guadalmina** (952 88 22 11) was being upgraded when we were in the area but it looks as if it will be exceptionally good. **Puerto Banus** is well situated and self-catering accommodation with golf packages can be found, such as at **Guitart Royal Gardens** in the Valle del Golf (952 81 31 25).

Where to Eat

Once again it is the restaurants frequented by locals that get our recommendation. Unfortunately, in the Costa del Sol area they are not so frequent and much pricier. Otherwise, you can dine like a king for 2000 pesetas. The tourist areas such as Fuengirola and Torremolinos are competitive but often the standards are not so high. In the north of the area near Almería, the **El Brillante Restaurante** is well signposted and seen from the *autopista* (950 48 09 41). It is almost a truck stop but they look after you with local panache. With the main fishing fleet operating out of **Málaga**, the town offers some of the best seafood eateries especially along the city beaches. For fine dining in Málaga try the **Parador Gibralfaro** (952 22 19 02). **La Alborada Restaurant** in Estepona (952 80 20 47) serves local and steak dishes to the highest standards. In Marbella, the **Santiago** (952 77 43 39) is ideal for seafood with a huge selection on offer.

Where to go

Málaga is an often-bypassed attraction in itself but it offers the **Picasso Museum** – Málaga was his birthplace. Check out also the **Alcazaba** and the **Gibralfaro Castle**. Further south, **Mijas village** is one of the most popular tourist outings but it gets crazily crowded between 10:00 and 20:00, with parking being a major problem. **Ronda** or any of the **Pueblos Blancos** (white villages) make for a nice drive into the interior – try to go on market day. Enjoy a meal in Marbella's old town, but **Puerto Banus** is the place to go for an evening of eating and sightseeing among the yacht crowd – famous faces are a no-cost extra. Otherwise, golfers will often be happy to relax by the pool or take a walk along the beach in between or after rounds. The laid-back lifestyle of the Costa del Sol soon affects you.

Tourist Information Offices

Almería Tourist Board
C/ Navarro Rodrigo, 17
Tel: 950 26 72 33
Fax: 950 26 75 45

Marbella Tourist Board
Glorieta de la Fontanilla 29600
Marbella
Tel: 952 77 14 42

Below: Glimpses of Old Spain still exist in Marbella's Old Town.

Chapter 4

Province of Cádiz

The Province of Cádiz overlooks the Mediterranean as well as the Atlantic Ocean. In the southeast of the region, the Sotogrande complex has been a privileged tourist and residential enclave for several decades and there are six excellent golf courses here. Meanwhile, to the north, the Atlantic coastal strip is just developing its resorts. These promise to be as attractive as their forerunners. The Seville area is generally a rather dignified tourist destination in itself, but a round can be had on one of several excellent nearby venues.

Visitors may find traffic problems in this area. From the Costa del Sol, the N340 *autopista* passes the town of Estepona and for some 25km (15 miles) reduces to a two-lane route. The extension linking the four-lane N340 with the motorway at Sotogrande is due to be built in 2002.

Sotogrande is very much like the Costa del Sol in terms of weather. It is sheltered and mild through the winter and cooled by seaside breezes through the summer. It is possible to play golf for most of the year, but is most popular with visitors in the winter months. February and March are becoming busy on the newer resorts of Cádiz as they are discovered by Northern Europeans seeking sunshine and sport. Through the summer months with cooling breezes from the Atlantic, there is perhaps more chance to enjoy golf on the new courses around Chiclana. The summer temperatures inland around Seville tend to be searing, so it is best to play early or late in the day to avoid the heat.

If you are in the area on business and feel like having an impromptu game of golf, telephone ahead to guarantee a tee time.

Left: Seville is one of the most stylish cities in Europe.
Above: Barrio de Santa Cruz in Seville is a warren of alleys and patios.

Sotogrande

Many visitors choose to arrive at Sotogrande and the Province of Cádiz via Gibraltar. Gibraltar Airport (Tel: 956 77 30 26) has excellent daily services from the UK and the Sotogrande courses are only 15 minutes' drive from 'The Rock'.

Since the Rock of Gibraltar was seized by the British in 1704, there have been frequent disputes over its sovereignty but, although Spanish workers entering and leaving Gibraltar sometimes face customs delays, this rarely causes disruption for tourists.

Sotogrande was established as a tourist enclave in the 1960s but it has been much slower to expand compared with other southern coastal regions in Spain. This has kept it more exclusive. Recent construction tends to be in keeping with a well-established high standard. There are currently one nine-hole and six 18-hole courses here, ranging from the world-famous Valderrama to the nine-hole municipal course at La Cañada Golf Club (both designed by Robert Trent Jones). Generally, Sotogrande is an expensive area to stay in and does not offer such a wide range of tourist facilities, but it is quiet and sophisticated with a wonderful marina and beach area.

Cádiz

The notorious N340 trundles on north through the largely agricultural region of Chiclana y La Janda. It is on Cádiz's coastal fringe, less than one hour's drive from Gibraltar, that attractive alternatives to Spain's more established coastal resorts are now being created. While residential construction is still very much in evidence, there are several good golf courses already available. The building of 27 holes at Novo Sancti Petri has been key

to this area's development and all three nine-hole sections are well worth sampling. Meanwhile, there are vast stretches of natural beaches, authentic fishing ports and genuine elements of Spain that you would have difficulty finding in more touristy areas.

The city of Cádiz is the capital of the Province of Cádiz. It is one of the oldest cities in Europe, made famous by its trade with America after the voyage of Christopher Columbus. It still exports large quantities of sherry wine, cork, olives, figs and salted fish. Cádiz is a beautiful city, especially near the harbour where there are imposing Moorish-style white buildings and wide promenades. Only a few kilometres north is the town of Jerez – English merchants corrupted this to 'Sherry' – and it is here that you can visit the finest Bodegas (wineries).

Seville

Seville is Spain's third largest city after Madrid and Barcelona. Most of the main tourist attractions are found in the city centre. The old Jewish quarter of Santa Cruz is quite charming, as is the Alcázar Palace, the Plaza del España and the cathedral. Seville is a centre for fashion and it is worth shopping in for both choice and keen prices. The Triana area, south of the river, is worth exploring for its flamenco bars – it was in Seville that the dance first developed. Golf is available on some five courses mostly to the south of the city. These are generally members' clubs, but visitors will be given tee times if a booking is made in advance.

One hundred kilometres (62 miles) further west is the city of Huelva. It was from here that Christopher Columbus set sail in 1492 to discover America. There are three courses in this corner.

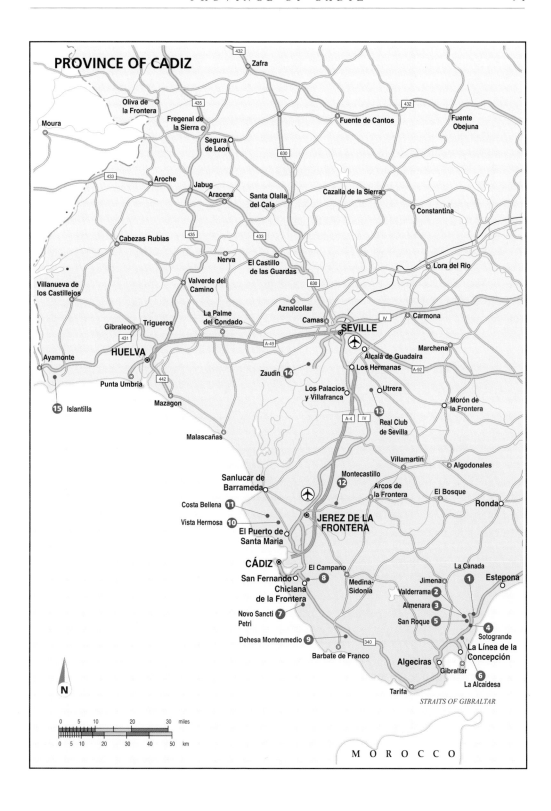

PROVINCE OF CADIZ

Zafra

Oliva de la Frontera

Moura

Fregenal de la Sierra

Fuente de Cantos

Fuente Obejuna

Segura de Leon

Aroche

Jabug

Aracena

Santa Olalla del Cala

Cazalla de la Sierra

Constantina

Cabezas Rubias

Nerva

El Castillo de las Guardas

Lora del Rio

Villanueva de los Castillejos

Valverde del Camino

Gibraleon

Trigueros

La Palme del Condado

Aznalcollar

Camas

SEVILLE

Carmona

HUELVA

Ayamonte

Marchena

Alcalá de Guadaira

Los Hermanas

Zaudin **14**

Punta Umbria

Mazagon

Los Palacios y Villafranca

Utrera

Morón de la Frontera

15 Islantilla

Malascañas

Real Club de Sevilla

Villamartin

Algodonales

Sanlucar de Barrameda

Montecastillo

12

Arcos de la Frontera

El Bosque

Ronda

Costa Bellena **11**

Vista Hermosa **10**

El Puerto de Santa Maria

JEREZ DE LA FRONTERA

CÁDIZ

El Campano

La Canada

San Fernando

8

Medina-Sidonia

Jimena

1 Estepona

Chiclana de la Frontera

Valderrama **2**

Almenara **3**

San Roque **5**

4

Sotogrande

Novo Sancti Petri **7**

Dehesa Montenmedio **9**

Barbate de Franco

Algeciras

Gibraltar

La Línea de la Concepción

6

La Alcaidesa

Tarifa

STRAITS OF GIBRALTAR

N

0 5 10 20 30 miles

0 5 10 20 30 40 50 km

M O R O C C O

The Ryder Cup

1997 marked a proud moment in Spanish golfing history. For the first time, the Ryder Cup, the historic team contest between the United States of America and Europe, was played on continental Europe at the southern Spanish course of Valderrama.

Staging a Ryder Cup is seen as a prestigious event on a national and international level. Many years of planning go into it.

The venue of Sotogrande in the south-west corner of Spain had already been acclaimed as one of the finest courses in Europe, having hosted the Volvo Masters tournament for eight years. Royalty, nobility and heads of state witnessed the Ryder Cup event, as did thousands of golf spectators from around the world. There were some 75 corporate jets parked at Málaga Airport and a further 25 in nearby Gibraltar, to say nothing of the five cruise liners docked at Algeciras. Meanwhile, President Bill Clinton personally sent the American team off.

For all of its prestige, the Ryder Cup has also become one of the most contentious events in professional golf. Europe had faired well, regaining the cup in 1995 at Oak Hill Country Club in Rochester, N.Y., a defeat that the Americans were still smarting from. The American team was favoured to win the three-day contest at Valderrama, but the match turned out to be nerve-racking and unpredictable.

After some unsettled and unseasonably wet weather during the first two days, the Europeans entered the final day with an apparently insurmountable five-point lead. 'Tom Kite threw everything at him at Valderrama,' said Colin Montgomerie of Seve Ballesteros' captaincy, 'and didn't succeed'. The Americans rallied until Bernhard Langer defeated Brad Faxon. This gave the Europeans at the very least a tie and retention of the title. Montgomerie clinched victory by courteously conceding his match for a half with Scott Hoch. The final score was Europe 14, United States 13.

The emotion elicited by a Ryder Cup win seems to surpass all similar events. This was certainly the case at Valderrama, although play never crossed into the realms of bad sportsmanship. Valderrama was seen as a success in every way and has since put Spanish golf firmly in the public eye.

Above: The victorious European team, captained by Seve Ballesteros, prepares a Ryder Cup toast. The emotion that surrounds a Ryder Cup win seems to surpass that at similar events.

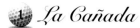 La Cañada

*La Cañada Golf Club, Ctra. Guadiaro, Guadiaro,
Cádiz, Andalucía*
TEL: *956 79 41 00* **FAX:** *956 79 44 11*
EMAIL: *canada@golf-andalucia.net*
LOCATION: *Near Sotogrande. From the N340 take the
road towards Guadiaro. It is well signposted.*
COURSE: *9 holes, 5746m/6284yd, par 70,
SSS 72*
GREEN FEES: *££*
FACILITIES: *Clubhouse, driving range, hand trolley
hire, pitching and putting green, golf tuition, club hire,
pro-shop, restaurant and bar.*
VISITORS: *Weekdays only. No visitors at weekend.*

Nearby to the courses of high-cost Valderrama and Sotogrande, La Cañada (pronounced La Canyada) is a casual and pleasant nine holes of reasonable character and reasonable price. If you are in the area and fancy an informal round, then La Cañada is ideal. Many expatriate residents in the area play here regularly if they don't have the game or perhaps the disposable funds to play at the more expensive nearby clubs.

However, La Cañada should not be written off by more serious golfers, as is indicated by the standard scratch. The course plays slightly uphill for the first two holes but it is an easy walk thereafter. The 4th is a blind tee shot over a rise. From here the view of the Mediterranean and Sotogrande is magnificent – but you might not see your ball again. There is a pond at the back of the green. Otherwise, if you place your drive well, this par 5 could be a safe birdie opportunity. The La Cañada greens are undulating and very fast. The last two holes are tricky, the 8th needing a punch well to the back of the green to stop the ball falling back into the water and the 9th plays dramatically over a deep, shrub-infested ravine. Don't even think about looking for it.

*Below: La Cañada is a good, yet keen-priced, test among
high-priced Sotogrande courses.*

 Valderrama

*Valderrama Golf Club, Ctra. de Cádiz, 11310
Sotogrande, Andalucía*
TEL: *956 79 12 00* **FAX:** *956 79 60 28*
WWW: *www.valderrama.com*
EMAIL: *the.manager@valderrama.com*
LOCATION: *Just off N340.*
COURSE: *18 holes, 6234m/6817yd, par 71, SSS 71*
GREEN FEES: *££££££££££*
FACILITIES: *Clubhouse, driving range, buggy hire,
hand trolley hire, pitching and putting greens, practice
bunker, club hire, pro-shop, restaurant and bar.*
VISITORS: *Visitors welcome weekdays and weekends
between 12 and 2pm (36-visitor rounds per day). A
handicap certificate of 24 for men and 32 for women will
be asked for. Soft spikes only.*

VALDERRAMA

HOLE	YD	M	PAR	HOLE	YD	M	PAR
1	389	356	4	10	389	356	4
2	399	365	4	11	547	500	5
3	173	158	3	12	212	194	3
4	535	489	5	13	402	368	4
5	381	348	4	14	370	338	4
6	163	149	3	15	225	206	3
7	460	421	4	16	422	386	4
8	344	315	4	17	511	467	5
9	441	403	4	18	454	415	4
OUT	3285	3004	35	IN	3532	3230	36

6817YD • 6234M • PAR 71

The Valderrama course at Sotogrande is one of the finest in Europe. It is a testing championship venue that has hosted the Volvo Masters, the Ryder Cup in 1997 and more recently the WGC American Express Championship.

The course's rise to world-wide prominence has been relatively quick. It started when tour professional Mel Pyatt convinced the complex's owner and president, Jaime Ortiz Patino, that Valderrama was suitable for hosting a European Tour event. So well did this end-of-season grand finale go that Valderrama (formerly Nuevo Sotogrande) went on to host the Volvo Masters for a further eight years. During this time, and most particularly during the course's greatest moment as host to the 1997 Ryder Cup, many great golfing moments have been witnessed.

Valderrama's rolling fairways, ancient trees, (some 500 years old) and its tight tee propositions will call for a virtual arsenal of shots. Commonly, if you have the game for it, you will be required to shape the ball around a hazard, inevitably a wide, stumpy cork tree. Otherwise, many players are forced to squander strokes simply nudging the ball back into a playable position. While the course presents such a league of difficulties there is one that cannot be predicted nor accounted for. The notorious Poniente wind can create horrifying cross-gusts that greatly magnify mistakes or indeed destroy a seemingly well-struck shot.

On approaching the greens, the lush fairways are ideal to impart backspin. This is useful if the green is small, as most of them are. Generally you will find that balls hold well,

especially at the early and late part of the year when the greens are still soft.

There are no mediocre holes to be had at Valderrama. The 4th is most memorable, indeed the course's signature. It is a straight-ahead par 5 that, if faced with a westerly wind, can be very long indeed. The tiny green is protected by a lake on the front right with a waterfall behind as well as an overhanging tree to the left.

The 17th is also notable, another par 5 with a fast green that can cause problems with backspin into the lake. This hole has been recently re-modified to bring it closer to the original Trent Jones design, although the swathe of rough that once inhabited the middle of the fairway has thankfully not returned.

Tour players testify that this course can bring out the best and worst of your game. Accuracy off the tees is paramount. Otherwise you will find cork oak trees or, at the very least, you will land in the fluffy Bermuda rough left 10cm high and close in to the fairway. It is best to play as safely as you can.

Above: Valderrama is notorious for its tight drives, with ancient cork oak trees and side winds causing most problems.

Since 1997 and the Ryder Cup event, the course seems to be finally settling. While it remains difficult, and sometimes quirky, it is a great and worthwhile challenge to golfers who relish playing the great tournament courses.

Below: Valderrama's off-course facilities rival the first-class conditions found out on the playing field.

 Almenara

Above: Set higher into the hills, Almenara has a more rolling terrain than its Sotogrande neighbours.

Almenara Golf Club, Avda. Los Cortijos s/n 11310, Andalucía
TEL: *956 79 01 11* **FAX:** *956 79 03 37*
EMAIL: *almenara@golf-andalucia.net*
LOCATION: *North of N340 at marker km132.*
COURSE: *18 holes, 6168m/6745yd, par 72, SSS 72*
GREEN FEES: *££££*
FACILITIES: *Hotel, clubhouse, driving range, buggy hire, hand trolley hire, pitching and putting greens, practice bunker, golf tuition, club hire, pro-shop, restaurant, bar and showers.*

The Sotogrande area has perhaps a leaning towards portentousness with some of its courses. It is not seen as a general golf tourism destination. The opening of the Almenara Hotel and Health Club, which is surrounded by its own golf course, is just the beginning of development to bring more golf tourists to the area. Only a mile or so north of the entrance to Valderrama and Sotogrande Old, the course plays over a series of lofty prominences; a golf cart therefore will help to smooth the progress of the experience.

Designed by Dave Thomas, the layout has two plainly perceptible segments. The front nine stretches out around and through fairly dense woodland, while the back nine is dominated by a large lake and stream that influences four holes. The 6th is a long narrow climb with a fairway that is the same width of the green in many areas. You should try to lay to the right off the tee and again into the green to avoid the large, long, left-side bunker.

The 13th is one of the few holes on the back nine not to feature water, but it is a tight dogleg with crucial bunkering at both sides of the corner. It is possible to fly the bunkers in a 'risk and reward' situation, but mistakes will cost dear and it is a small fairway on which to land with a driver. The second shot could require as much as 220m/240yd up to a wide green.

Sotogrande

*Sotogrande Golf Club, Ctra. Cádiz-Málaga, km130
11310 Sotogrande, Andalucía*
TEL: *956 79 50 50* **FAX:** *956 79 50 29*
WWW: *golfsotogrande.com*
EMAIL: *sotogrande@golf-andalucia.net*
LOCATION: *Off the N340, turn south into the well-marked Sotogrande (gated) estate.*
COURSE: *18 holes, 5853m/6400yd, par 72, SSS 72*
GREEN FEES: *££££££*
FACILITIES: *Clubhouse, driving range, buggy hire, hand and electric trolley hire, pitching and putting greens, practice bunker, club repair, club hire, caddy, pro-shop, restaurant, bar, children's playground, swimming pool, tennis courts and showers.*
VISITORS: *Between 11:00–13:00 only and handicaps required; 25 for men and 30 for Ladies.*

Sotogrande Old is expensive and slightly restricted to visitors, although those who book well in advance will have no trouble in securing certain tee times.

The course's beauty is in the wide expanses of fairway with little rough to worry about. There is plenty of character in the course, which features lakes and trees as well as the

Below: The course at Sotogrande Old offers wide expanses of fairway, with judiciously placed hazards.

occasional raised green, but many find they have an excellent round using their drivers, long irons and wedges on a regular basis.

There are lovely, flowing lines to this course interrupted by the stands of palm or chaparro trees, which are bent and gnarled. Generally it is an easy-walking course apart from the tough section on the homeward stretch.

The clubhouse has been totally refurbished recently, but has kept its original southern Andalucian style. There is a great camaraderie around the clubhouse.

The 7th plays downhill, a par 4 with water to the right and an artfully arduous arrangement of trees and bunkers. The 12th through 17th all feature water and comprise the most difficult section of the Old Course. The 13th is an easy par 3, while the 14th is a par 5 over the lake. Most people play towards the bunker on the right, but it is actually better to play left; the fairway is wider than it looks from the tee. It's a tight approach on this hole, usually playing two more clubs than would normally be considered. If your game is on by this section you could score well, but bear in mind that at Sotogrande it is the greens that count and putting is never easy.

 *San Roque*

San Roque Golf Club, N340 km127, San Roque, Andalucía
TEL: *956 61 30 30* **FAX:** *956 61 30 12*
EMAIL: *sanroque@golf-andalucia.net*
LOCATION: *Off the N340, about 20km before La Línea.*
COURSE: *18 holes, 6048m/6614yd, par 72, SSS 72*
GREEN FEES: *££££*
FACILITIES: *Hotel, clubhouse, driving range, buggy hire, hand trolley hire, putting green, practice bunker, golf tuition, club repair, club hire, caddy, pro-shop, bar, restaurant, swimming pool, tennis courts, sauna and showers, and equestrian centre.*

San Roque is an elegant oasis of golf and leisure. The course was fashioned around the former home of the Domecq family and its *meseta* (farmhouse and farm). Designed by Dave Thomas with input from fellow Ryder Cup player, Tony Jacklin, the course offers a considerable challenge in length and strategy, along with excellent views over Southern Andalucía.

The course's length is moderated and made far more comfortable from the forward tees for higher handicaps. Do not feel self-conscious using the forward tees if you are playing over 18 handicap as otherwise the course may prove too difficult and demoralizing.

Apart from several tight situations on the front nine, the fairways are wide and sheltered by surrounding trees. Its setting on a level valley floor makes for easy walking. The back nine is noted for water hazards and the exposed 13th and 15th holes, which rise and fall over a hill. Apart from these, the holes to watch out for are the 8th and 18th. The final hole has water to the left and a long carry over the lake and stream. Strategic play is everything here.

Generally San Roque will test every part of the game, particularly off the tees and into the greens. The greens are large and undulating and usually very nippy. The combination of an excellent hotel at the Suites with its leisure facilities and accommodating golf course (off the forward tees) makes San Roque attractive to corporate groups as well as to tourists.

Below: San Roque is a complete golf escape, with the Suites Hotel on site and overlooking the course.

Above: Alcaidesa offers a different golfing experience than
that of its Sotogrande neighbours.

 ## *Alcaidesa*

*Alcaidesa Links Golf Club, N340 km124.6 11600,
La Línea, Andalucía*
Tel: *956 79 10 40* **Fax:** *956 79 10 41*
Email: *alcaidesa@golf-andalucia.net*
Location: *At km124.6 on the N340, turn southeast
towards the sea.*
Course: *18 holes, 6158m/6734yd, par 72,
SSS 72*
Green Fees: *££££*
Facilities: *Clubhouse, driving range, buggy hire,
hand trolley hire, pitching and putting greens, practice
bunker, club repair, club hire, pro-shop, restaurant, bar
and showers.*

Situated on the coast between La Línea and
Estepona, Alcaidesa enjoys fabulous views
across the Mediterranean.

Some might say that Alcaidesa has
delusions of grandeur that have rubbed off
from its more illustrious neighbours such as
Valderrama and Sotogrande. It also sells itself
as Spain's only true links course. Admittedly
the course has improved tremendously since it
was opened in 1992, with a major revamp in
1999, but moderate your expectations and

you will enjoy this perfectly adequate course
all the better.

Along with overall improvements, the
course has been lengthened, with the 15th
now an excellent par 5. Combine the greater
length with the warm winds that blow along
the coast and the strips of thick, heathery
rough and you could be put in mind of a
Scottish links. However, there are innate
differences. The turf is quite dissimilar, lacking
that crisp, tweedy knit that you find on links
courses and the fairway undulations are not
so influential.

Nevertheless, Alcaidesa is coming into its
prime and forms a diverse experience to most
of the courses in the Sotogrande corner. It is
also worth mentioning the magnificent views
available on the course, such as the Rock of
Gibraltar and the Atlas Mountains in not-so-
far-off North Africa.

⑦ *Novo Sancti Petri*

Novo Sancti Petri Golf Club, Urb. Novo Sancti Petri,
11139 Chiclana de la Frontera, Andalucía
TEL: *956 49 40 05* **FAX:** *956 49 43 50*
WWW: *golf-novosancti.es*
EMAIL: *sales@golf-novosancti.es*
LOCATION: *Off the N340 towards Cádiz, about an*
hour from Sotogrande, signposted towards the coast.
COURSE: *27 holes, 6169m/6746yd, par 72, SSS 72*
GREEN FEES: *££££*
FACILITIES: *Clubhouse, driving range, buggy hire,*
hand and electric trolley hire, putting green, practice
bunker, golf tuition, club repair, club hire, caddy, pro-
shop, restaurant, bar, children's playground, tennis
courts, horse riding, sauna and showers.
VISITORS: *Visitors welcome weekdays and weekends.*
Soft spikes only.

If you want a change from the Costa del Sol head for Chiclana. The golf facilities of Novo Sancti Petri are part of an expanding estate found halfway between Sotogrande and the city of Cádiz. Much of the interior of this area is set for residential development, but behind La Barrosa beach and opposite the golf course is a selection of excellent hotels.

In the late 1980s when Novo Sancti Petri's designer, Seve Ballesteros, began the surveying

Above: Novo Sancti Petri's 27 holes offer a wide variety of golfing challenges, from thick tree-lined parkland to open links.

work, the terrain was found to be ideally suited for three very different layouts. The resulting three nine-hole tracts, while similar in length and each par 36, are quite diverse. The first nine, *El Mar*, offers lakes and gently rolling terrain that opens on to sea views. This section has a distinctive links base especially for its seaside holes. The 4th is the most notable, a par 4 with an elevated, dome-shaped green that is regularly approached into a stiff westerly wind.

The *Centro* course seems longer than the others, but the *Pinos* course is the most difficult, and would seem almost impossible from the white tees. Visitors (from forward tees) find it manageable, although the holes are long and confined by tall umbrella pines that play havoc with any drive that is a ball-width short of perfect. Wind coming off the Atlantic or the warmer Levante wind from the southeast can influence all three sections and is a regular feature.

8 El Campano

El Campano Golf Club, Ctra Cádiz-Málaga, km14.7
11130 Chiclana de la Frontera, Andalucía
TEL: *956 23 00 20* **FAX:** *956 40 21 34*
EMAIL: *elcampano@golf-andalucia.net*
LOCATION: *On the N340 Cádiz–Málaga, km14.7.*
COURSE: *9 holes, 3072m/3360yd, par 70, SSS 70*
GREEN FEES: *££*
FACILITIES: *Clubhouse, driving range, hand trolley hire, pitching and putting greens, practice bunker, golf tuition, club repair, club hire, pro-shop, restaurant, bar, swimming pool, tennis court and showers.*

Campano is an easy-going nine-holer. It has proved attractive to retired Northern Europeans who built their retirement villas here, many overlooking the course. The fairways are flat and narrow and call for short placement shots, ideal for senior players who regularly beat their younger contenders.

There is little trouble to encounter apart from the many pine and olive trees. Wind, however, can be more troublesome and on some days, particularly in the afternoon, the warm Levante can transform this mild-mannered course into a mischievous imp.

There is a fair amount of water in play such as at the 2nd, 3rd, 4th and 9th, again calling for strategic play.

9 Dehesa Montenmedio

Dehesa Montenmedio Golf Club, N340 km42.5,
11150 Vejer de la Frontera, Andalucía
TEL: *956 32 46 48* **FAX:** *956 23 24 43*
EMAIL: *montenmedio@golf-andalucia.net*
LOCATION: *On the N340 turn off at km42.5 towards the west.*
COURSE: *18 holes, 5897m/6449yd, par 71, SSS 71*
GREEN FEES: *£££££*
FACILITIES: *Clubhouse, driving range, buggy hire, hand trolley hire, pitching and putting greens, practice bunker, golf tuition, club hire, pro-shop, restaurant, bar and showers. Tee times have been initially restricted so telephone well in advance.*

Designed by Alejandro Maldonado, the course plays through a natural amphitheatre of pine and cork trees with a comfortable distance and plenty of grassy landing areas between them. Club golfers will be comfortable here and indeed the designer seems to have created a course to fit the players that will use it – a rare talent these days.

Wind can make a lot of difference and this coast has its fair share. However, most players will come off Montenmedio pleased with themselves and the course. It is a flattering layout for most players, in very good condition. The off-course facilities are equally good, so stay for a meal after your round.

GIBRALTAR

If you are in the Sotogrande area, a trip to the 'Rock' is a must. Gibraltar's novelty lies in its lofty limestone crag, its population of Barbery apes and its cheap cigarettes and drink. It is a curious place with street names such as 'Bishop Rapallos Ramp' or pubs like 'The Angry Friar'. Its main street sports many British high street shops, tea rooms and pubs catering mainly for the British soldiers living and working here. Apart from such touches of English quaintness and the view of the harbour from the top of the Rock, it is not an overly attractive place. Nor are its Spanish neighbouring towns of La Línea and Algeciras. It is curious that there are few or perhaps no signs pointing the way to Gibraltar in its neighbouring town of La Línea, an indication of the strained relationship between the Spanish government and the British – but just keep heading towards the Rock, which can be seen everywhere. Bringing a car into Gibraltar might seem easy enough and it is easy to cross the border into the enclave but beware that the street system is not easy to get off and parking seems non-existent. Park away from the centre and then walk the mile or so into town.

Vista Hermosa

Vista Hermosa Golf Club, Urb. Vistahermosa,
Casa Grande, 11500 El Puerto de Santa María,
Andalucía
TEL: *956 54 19 68* **FAX:** *956 87 56 04*
EMAIL: *vistahermosa@golf-andalucia.net*
LOCATION: *1.5km from el Puerto de Santa María in*
la Bahia de Cádiz.
COURSE: *9 holes, 2746m/3000yd, par 72,*
SSS 70
GREEN FEES: *££££*
FACILITIES: *Clubhouse, driving range, hand trolley*
hire, putting green, golf tuition, club repair, club hire,
pro-shop, restaurant, bar, children's playground,
swimming pool, tennis court, horse riding, sauna
and showers.

This is a good old club worth a casual visit if you are around Cádiz. It is dominated by its keen membership, but is also visitor-friendly so call ahead to make sure of a tee time.

The most striking feature of the course is its clubhouse, a tall hybrid of a design somewhere between a Tudor half-timber of middle England and a Swiss chalet.

The course is short and defiant, with tight corners and stands of tall pines. Wind, as on any part of this coast, will transform the game. The 4th is a cracker, a par 4 with an island green. The 7th and the 9th are also worth looking out for. It's a challenging little gem and worth visiting both for the course and for the general ambience of the club.

Below: One of the most striking elements of Vista
Hermosa is its clubhouse.

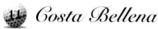 Costa Bellena

*Costa Bellena Golf Club, Ctra. Rota–Chipiona km21,
11520 Rota, Andalucía*
TEL: *956 84 70 70* **FAX:** *956 84 70 50*
WWW: *bellenagolf.com*
EMAIL: *costa@bellenagolf.com*
LOCATION: *20km west from Jerez on the 604
Rota–Chipiona road.*
COURSE: *18 holes, 6187m/6766yd, par 72, SSS 71*
GREEN FEES: *££*
FACILITIES: *Clubhouse, big driving range, covered
driving range, buggy hire, hand trolley hire, pitching and
putting greens, practice bunker, club hire, pro-shop,
restaurant and bar.*

Costa Bellena is another new development
on the Andalucian–Atlantic coast. It is as
yet undiscovered – but judging by the
apartments being built overlooking the course
this situation will not last long. Depending on
availability of flights into Jerez, Costa Bellena
could be an ideal alternative to golf courses on
the Mediterranean coast. Several good hotels
are available in the area, and there are plenty
of local restaurants serving excellent food,
particularly fish dishes.

*Above: The Costa Bellena course looks set to mature into
a first-class test.*

The course, designed by José María
Olazábal, is long and dry. The Bermuda
fairways are smooth and the greens fast. From
the tees, the course presents good definition
with newly planted palms and 100-year-old
transplanted olive trees. High-handicap players
will find no difficulty playing to their level, as
the course is set up to avoid punishing
situations. Good golfers will find its
combination of length and the interesting
situation of most greens a challenge. The 13th
can be the most difficult into a wind with the
green lower than the fairway and two
gathering bunkers to the left. The 18th is the
most memorable, a long hole with a lake
fringing the last stretch. Like many of the holes
on this course, the green approach kinks right
disallowing a running approach.

A nine-hole par 3 as well as a huge driving
range and greenside practice area makes this a
good venue for game-improvement.

Montecastillo

Montecastillo Golf Club and Resort, Ctra. de Arcos,
11406 Jerez de la Frontera, Andalucía
TEL: *956 15 12 00* **FAX:** *956 15 12 09*
WWW: *www.montecastillo.com*
EMAIL: *markt@montecastillo.com*

LOCATION: *From Jerez take the N342 east; it is well
signposted.*
COURSE: *18 holes, 6456m/7060yd, par 72,
SSS 72*
GREEN FEES: *£££££*
FACILITIES: *Clubhouse, driving range, covered
driving range, buggy hire, hand trolley hire,
pitching and putting greens, practice bunker, golf tuition,
club repair, club hire, pro-shop, restaurant, bar,
swimming pool, tennis court, horse riding, fitness
centre, sauna, Jacuzzi and showers.*

MONTECASTILLO

HOLE	YD	M	PAR	HOLE	YD	M	PAR
1	387	354	4	10	410	375	4
2	221	202	3	11	234	214	3
3	564	516	5	12	522	477	5
4	381	348	4	13	424	388	4
5	416	380	4	14	172	157	3
6	413	378	4	15	464	424	4
7	432	395	4	16	517	473	5
8	190	174	3	17	374	342	4
9	517	473	5	18	422	386	4
OUT	3521	3220	36	IN	3534	3236	36

7060YD • 6456M • PAR 72

Montecastillo is often voted among the best 50 courses in Europe and its adjoining hotel/resort one of the best 100 Golf Hotel Resorts in the World. It is also a regular host of the Volvo Masters.

Jack Nicklaus, the course designer, went to great lengths to ensure that players always had a look at where they were hitting on this course and so great teeing mounds have been created to look down on the long surging fairways. As the land is quite rolling, on most occasions he was helped in this purpose. In this way it is an honest course, in that you get what you play – except perhaps for the 13th, which doglegs right out of sight.

The 3rd is a good par 5 with a large bunker and scrub to catch over-ambitious drives. On the left of a tapered fairway is a smaller bunker that does surprising damage. The green is also heavily defended left, with marshes to the right. Unless you are confident of clearing trouble, play the hole safely for a confident par. The 15th is a long, uphill par 4 with a carry over a dense ravine. The challenge comes in the second shot, which has to cover the incline and reach a slim plateau green.

Generally, the front nine is wider and fairly straightforward, while the terrain of the back nine deserves a more complicated ranking. Nicklaus has made advantage of this and any player will feel thoroughly tested.

The course is generally characterised by small sparse trees, a lot of mounding on fairway sides and raised and well defended greens. The

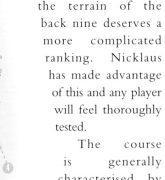

bunkers are a particular feature with multiple colonies of exaggerated shapes placed in the most effective positions. Winds also range over this high and exposed course.

Nicklaus seems to constantly goad players into stretching their games with this design, and many players come off quite proud if they have risen to the challenge.

The castellated clubhouse and its adjoining hotel are luxuriously appointed and offer all sorts of after-golf diversions.

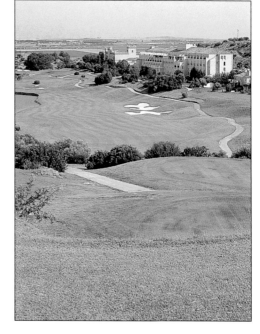

Right: The 18th hole at Montecastillo provides an excellent finish to a challenging and enjoyable course.
Below: Bunkering is a major consideration at Montecastillo.

13 Sevilla

Real Club de Golf Sevilla, 41089 Montequinto,
Seville, Andalucía
TEL: *954 12 43 01* **FAX:** *954 12 42 29*
LOCATION: *3km south from Seville on the*
Seville–Utrera road.
COURSE: *18 holes, 6049m/6615yd, par 72,*
SSS 72
GREEN FEES: *££*
FACILITIES: *Clubhouse, driving range, covered*
driving range, buggy hire, hand and electric trolley
hire, pitching and putting greens, practice bunker,
club repair, club hire, pro-shop, restaurant, bar and
showers.

Above: Sevilla was designed by José María Olazábal.

José María Olazábal can take the credit for creating this excellent test of golf. It is a bit of a hybrid. The flat terrain has been well worked to create the course that he envisaged, but the end result is a demanding series of great-playing golf holes that the competitive player will relish.

The team of greenkeepers seem to be up to speed and modifications to this decade-old course have only brought it closer to perfection. With stadium mounding all around the fairways and greens it would make a good European Tour venue given a little more length. A total of 96 bunkers and eight lakes defend the rolling topography, a tough but fair proposition.

Most of the longer holes require distance off the tee and precision into the smallish greens. The 2nd, for instance, is wide but you need to be long and straight to cover the 409m/447yd in two. The 6th is a tricky par 4 that doglegs left with two lakes on the left calling for a set-up position to the right in order to see the green and avoid the water. The 10th is typical of the greens, with discreet swales capable of carrying the ball yards from its target.

Olazábal is an excellent iron player and he has built this course to suit that style of game. The course is perhaps not the prettiest venue – there are no hills or groves of trees – but it certainly fulfils the needs of good golfers.

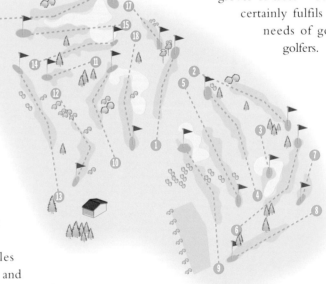

 ## Zaudín

Zaudín Golf Club, Ctra. Bormujos Mairena km1.5,
Tomares, Andalucía
TEL: *954 15 33 44* **FAX:** *954 15 41 59*
LOCATION: *Off the road Mairena–Tomares, km1.5.*
COURSE: *18 holes, 5869m/6418yd, par 71, SSS 71*
GREEN FEES: *££££*
FACILITIES: *Clubhouse, driving range, covered driving range, buggy hire, hand and electric trolley hire, putting green, practice bunker, club repair, club hire, pro-shop, restaurant and bar.*

Zaudín is Gary Player's most lauded Spanish project. Palm, orange and olive trees define the wide fairways along with a fair spattering of water.

There is a great variety to the holes. The 3rd offers a lake to be carried with out of bounds to the right. Next, the 4th, at 492m/538yd, is the longest on the course. Off the tee, the way is plain, but it is the excellent use of bunkers and water that changes the game and approach shots have to be planned for and expertly executed. The greens are moderate, but not a give-away, with plenty of sand to defend themselves. The two closing holes are interesting. The 17th, a par 4, plays from a raised tee towards water then over the lake to a tiny green with two bunkers behind. The threat of water ahead and left often forces players into the rear bunkers. The 18th is another tremendous challenge with water along the entire left flank. However you play the drive, the approach can still hit the skids as the lake bites in front left of the green.

Above: Gary Player was delighted with his creation at Zaudín Golf Course.

 ## Islantilla

Islantilla Golf Club, Urb. Islantilla, 21410 Isla
Cristina, Andalucía
TEL: *959 48 60 39* **FAX:** *959 48 61 04*
EMAIL: *isgolf@arrakis.es*
LOCATION: *Following the motorway A49 west from Seville, exit for Ayamonte, km80.*
COURSE: *18 holes, 5697m/6230yd, par 72, SSS 71*
GREEN FEES: *£££*
FACILITIES: *Clubhouse, driving range, buggy hire, hand and electric trolley hire, pitching and putting greens, practice bunker, golf tuition, club repair, club hire, pro-shop, restaurant, bar, swimming pool, sauna and showers.*

Set only a few kilometres from the Portugese/Spanish border, you may find yourself backtracking from Portugal to sample this southern Spanish delight. Most who encounter it tend to be converted. Designed by Enrique and José Canales with Luis Recaséns, there are 27 holes on offer. The Turespaña Masters Open de Andalucía has called by to give it their stamp of approval.

Overlooking the Atlantic Ocean, the course is essentially a parkland with hundreds of hoary old trees, wide fairways and large greens. Beyond this is ravaging rough, but you need to be well off-line to find yourself in this much trouble. No one forgets the 12th hole, a snaking dogleg that requires some steering off the tee. But before you take that on, stop and enjoy the incomparable view over the Atlantic. The 13th is also a teaser, a short but defiant par 5 that plays along the cliffs.

REGIONAL DIRECTORY

Where to Stay

If you are in the southern corner of the Province of Cádiz, the area known as Sotogrande, the top place for golfers is the four-star **San Roque Club's Suites Hotel** (956 61 30 30). Not only do you have the supreme San Roque course surrounding you but easy access to all of the area's renowned courses. With beautiful Arab architecture, the hotel has 64 rooms along with a sauna, swimming pool and shops. A good alternative is the **Almenara Hotel and Health Club** (956 790 306) also with its own course. The four-star **Club Maritimo Sotogrande** (956 79 02 00) is set overlooking the marina with restaurants and some shops nearby. It offers golf packages with reductions on local green fees.

On the Atlantic Coast near Chiclana is the **Hotel Meliá Sancti Petri** (956 49 12 00), a five-star operation between the golf courses and the beach with an excellent swimming pool. If you are playing the renowned Montecastillo course you may wish to stay at the on-site **Montecastillo Hotel and Golf Resort** (956 15 12 00). Alternatively, in Jerez there are many cheaper options such as the four-star **Hotel Royal Sherry Park** (956 30 30 11).

Seville is a wonderful city and it is worth staying close to the centre to enjoy its ambience then travel out to the golf courses. **The Alfonso XIII** (954 22 28 50) in San Fernando is an experience in itself. Near Islantilla Golf Club is the **Confortel Islantilla** with some 350 rooms (959 486 017).

Where to Eat

In Sotogrande, **El Barlevento Tapas Bar and Restaurant** (956 79 03 70) has a wide-ranging menu – try the sea bream or sole. There are two good restaurants in San Roque, **Los Remos** (956 69 84 12) and **Pedro** (956 69 84 53).

The city of Cádiz is renowned for its seafood and chilled gazpacho soup. A trip into town for a night out is well rewarded at restaurants such as **Meson El Copo** (956 67 77 10) and particularly **El Faro** (956 21 10 68). Further south, near to Novo Sancti Petri, is the township of Chiclana, where excellent local dishes are found in the numerous restaurants. If you are in a hurry, try the **Novo Golf Gachito** (956 49 52 49) near the course, but do not be afraid to venture further.

What to Do

The **Sotogrande** area is fairly quiet. There are some restaurants and shops surrounding the two

Below: Sotogrande Marina is elegant and the mooring place of many opulent yachts.

marinas, but it has none of the razzmatazz of Marbella or Puerto Banus further up the coast. **Gibraltar** is good for shopping. It can be busy and a bit grubby – but worth a look. Don't bother with the trip up **the Rock** unless you like being harangued by troops of greedy monkeys. If you are a windsurfer or like wide, windy beaches then head for **Tarifa** on the other side of Algeciras. Morocco and its Rif Mountains are clearly visible from here. The golf resorts on the **Costa de la Luz** are still developing.

Cádiz was one of the world's most important trading ports and has been for some 3000 years. Its springtime carnival is undoubtedly one of Spain's most elaborate. Surrounding the city are many natural parks and reserves. **Jerez** is the sherry capital of the world and the Bodegas of **Gonzalez Byassa and Pedro Domecq** are well worth visiting – but there are many more.

Sanlúcar is the seaside escape for Seville families and there are many good restaurants along the front. The area is famed for its vineyards.

Seville is a world unto itself, elegant and elevating. It epitomises many Spanish clichés with its bullfighting and flamenco, but in a way that is so proud and chic that you are soon converted. Check out the 14th-century **Alcázar** and the surrounding **Barrio de Santa Cruz,** a labyrinth of narrow lanes. The entire city is captivating.

Above: Barbary apes still dominate the Rock of Gibraltar.
Below: Petri, near Chiclana de la Frontera.

Chapter 5

Central & Northern Spain

The golfing visitor will find that from Extremadura north to the Atlantic coast there are fewer golf courses than in the more popular golfing regions to the south and on the islands. However, this situation is changing.

Golf in Madrid itself is largely the domain of the city's most affluent citizens. These clubs tend to be private, with large memberships (often of more than 1000), and a correspondingly high demand for tee times. For the visitor, Madrid is one of the most difficult cities in Europe in which to find a game of golf. Some of the members' clubs allow green fee players, but only at the discretion of the starter or caddy-master and depending on factors such as members' competitions. We found only four clubs in the Madrid area that would

Left: The Guggenheim Museum in Bilbao is an architectural tour de force. Above: The caddy store at San Sebastián was originally the Olazábal family home.

allow visitors rounds (without a member). On the north coast the situation improves notably, and it is possible to organise a varied and interesting golfing itinerary. The Basque region, Cantabria, Asturias and Galicia all have a reasonable selection of courses.

Madrid

Madrid is a flamboyant and stylish capital city. The architecture is perhaps not world-class, but the city has many artistic and cultural highlights. It is also a gregarious city. Restaurants, tapas bars and nightclubs are lively and stay open into the early hours.

Madrid is also the world capital of bullfighting, and locals and (indeed most of the nation) follow the televised events much like any other sport. It may be difficult to understand and accept such a cruel activity, but bullfighting is very much part of the Spanish psyche. Gaining some insight into

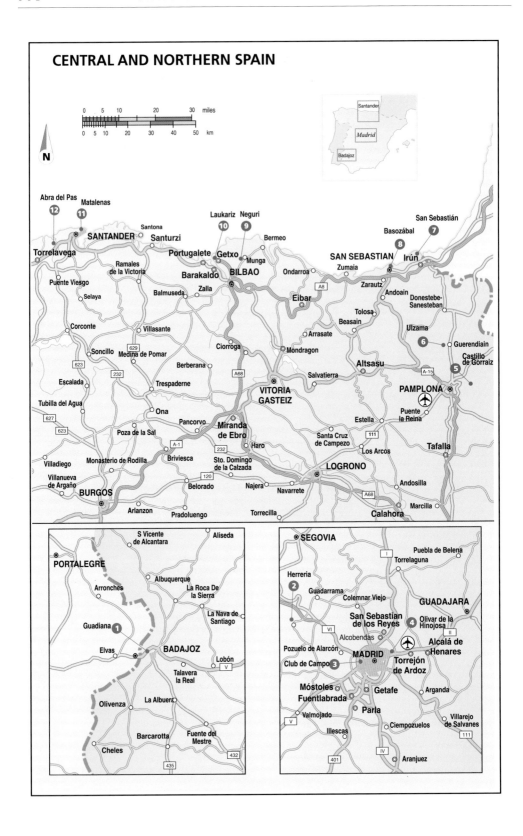

it can help illuminate the deep-rooted character and traditions of Spanish society. Madrid is also a shopper's delight and a good base for trips to many of the delightful historic towns of Castile.

The North Coast

If you approach the Spanish north coast by air into Santiago, Bilbao, San Sebastián or Santander you will realise why this area is called 'Green Spain'. Lush vegetation blankets steep mountain-sides with red pantiled villages contrasting in the valley floors. There is a good reason for so much greenery – rain. More than any other part of Spain, the north coast reaps the consequences of being bordered by the Atlantic Ocean and the turbulent Bay of Biscay.

'Green Spain' combines the areas of Galicia, Asturias, Cantabria and the Basque Country. Although the region stretches some 1000km (620 miles), it enjoys similar traits in climate, cuisine and tourist attractions, namely, mountains, sea, water sports and rural tourism. Golf features increasingly, although compared to other parts of the country courses are still quite sparse.

A noteworthy element throughout northern Spain and inland is the outstanding gastronomy. On the north coast, you will find fantastic seafood. Traditional dishes are simple and hearty. The vast range of cheeses is also remarkable. And of course Spain's most hearty vino tinto, La Rioja, is produced in the La Rioja valley inland from the coast.

Bilbao, the centre of the Basque country and a leading commercial port, is also now becoming known as a centre of the arts and culture, especially because of the world-class Guggenheim Museum, which opened in 1997.

Many of the courses in this area are private, catering to a large and well-heeled membership, but visitors are often welcome in the week.

For golf touring purposes, the area is probably best divided into two parts: the courses in the east from San Sebastián to

Below: Guadiana is a most welcoming club in the south-west corner of Extremadura.

Santander; and Galicia. It is also worth considering the area between Biarritz in the southwest corner of France and the San Sebastián corner of Basque Spain. There are a dozen good courses available here, all within a short driving distance.

Galicia Area

Galicia, the rugged, secluded corner of northwest Spain was, in a way, the country's first tourist destination when thousands of pilgrims walked the Pilgrim's Way to the holy shrine of St James at Santiago de Compostela. As a golf destination, the area has not yet reached such proportions of popularity, but with new courses being built and an increasing awareness of the delights of this, it might soon be attracting attention.

Santiago is the main town, with Pontevedra and Vigo on the coast to the south. There are some 20 golf courses in Galicia, with an increasing infrastructure for both tourism and golf. Otherwise, there are plenty of water sports on offer.

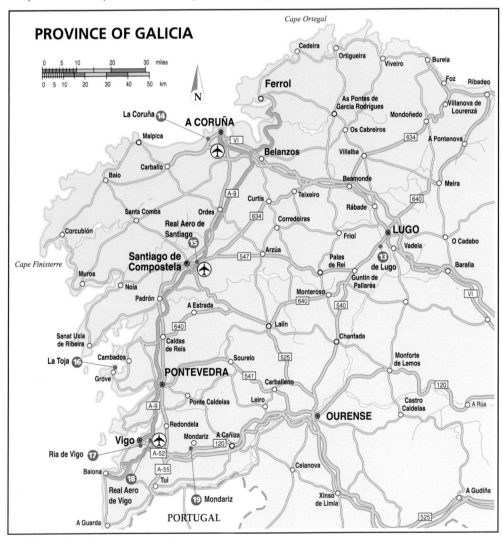

Guadiana

*Guadiana Golf Club, Ctra. Madrid–Lisbon, km393,
06080 Badajoz, Extremadura*
TEL: *924 44 81 88* **FAX:** *924 44 80 33*
LOCATION: *On the Madrid–Lisbon route just south of
Badajoz.*
COURSE: *18 holes, 6381m/6978yd, par 72,
SSS 72*
GREEN FEES: *££*
FACILITIES: *Clubhouse, driving range, buggy hire,
hand trolley hire, putting green, practice bunker, golf
tuition, club hire, pro-shop, restaurant, bar, billiard
room, swimming pool, tennis court, squash, fitness centre,
sauna and weekend nursery.*

This is a most welcoming club in the southwest corner of Extremadura near the Spanish/Portuguese border, around 400km (249miles) from Madrid. The course can be long and quite difficult but it is mostly on the level, so an easy stroll is in store.

Seven lakes in all come into play on 11 of the 18 holes, usually flanking two holes at a time. A stream crosses the 9th and 10th, particularly affecting the approach shots on the 9th. This is an excellent hole where you need to drive well in order to pitch over the water and on to the green. Lay-ups can be a little risky. The 10th flies the same stream, but it is not really a threat. However, this long par 4 takes some good golfing to reach the green in regulation.

Two other excellent holes are the 1st and 16th. The 1st is a stiff opener, a long par 5 with a left dogleg and water in front of the green. Palm trees and bunkers are strategically placed, so you need all your game to deal with this early challenge. The 16th is a medium-length par 3 with water in front of the green that sits high on a platform.

In spite of its flatness, Guadiana presents an excellent and enjoyable test of golf. It is a golfer's course with lots of challenges for practised players, but the casual high handicapper will also appreciate its design.

*Below: On Guadiana's course seven lakes come into play
on eleven holes.*

Herrería

*Herrería Golf Club, Ctra. Robledo de Chavela s/n,
28200 Madrid*
TEL: *918 90 51 11*
FAX: *918 90 71 54*
LOCATION: *Take the N VI Autopista to
junction 47 and then turn left towards la Sierra del
Guadarrama. When you get to San Lorenzo
de El Escorial, the entrance is 500m on the left
side.*
COURSE: *18 holes, 6050m/6616yd, par 72,
SSS 72*
GREEN FEES: *££££*
FACILITIES: *Driving range, trolley hire, putting green,
practice bunker, golf tuition, club hire, pro-shop,
restaurant, bar and showers.*

Although some 50km (30 miles) from
Madrid, Herreria is a public course, and,
in an area almost devoid of golfing
opportunities (because of the plethora of
private golf clubs), a most welcome one.
The Monasterio de San Lorenzo overlooks
the course, which in turn overlooks the
plain of la Meseta Central. Herrería
therefore has much to offer scenically as well
as sportingly.

The course plays over two distinct
halves. The front nine tends to be thickly
lined with oak trees, while the back nine is
much more open and airy with views over
the valley.

There is a great variety of holes here, so
you will feel well tested, with an occasion to
use every club in your bag. Trees and bunkers
dictate some strategic play, but you can still
open your shoulders and let the drives fly
when appropriate.

The 2nd hole is a very tricky par 5
with a blind second shot, a tight dogleg to
the right. The scenery starts at the 12th,
which is an easy par 4, and continues for the
next few holes. The 18th is an excellent par 4
to finish.

For a busy public course, Herrería is worth
seeking out for a round.

Club de Campo

Club de Campo, Carretera de Castilla, 28040 Madrid
TEL: *915 50 2010* **FAX:** *915 50 20 23*
LOCATION: *Northwest of Madrid on Castilla route.*
COURSE: *18 holes, 6335m/6928yd, par 72,
SSS 72*
GREEN FEES: *££££*
FACILITIES: *Clubhouse, driving range, covered driving
range, buggy hire, hand and electric trolley hire, pitching
and putting green, practice bunker, golf tuition, club
repair, club hire, pro-shop, restaurant, bar and showers.*

Club de Campo must be one of the
biggest sports clubs in Europe, located
just on the outskirts of Madrid. With more
than 12,000 members, there are many
activities on offer, including an equestrian
centre, hockey and tennis. There are also two
good 18-hole golf courses.

The main course is a fine example of Javier
Arana's design work. There is a problem of
over-demand and therefore considerable
pressure on the course, particularly the greens.
This is a council-run operation and the
greenkeeping staff do an admirable job, but
more radical upkeep, in fact relaying of some
greens, would be the best solution. Yet again,
in a city with very few opportunities for the
visitor to strike a ball on a genuinely good
layout, it would be churlish to complain.

LOCAL HEROES

Two figures have helped draw attention to
the region; Severiano Ballesteros, who grew
up and learned his craft on the hilly fairways
of Pedrena Golf Club near Santander, and
José María Olazábal, whose childhood home is
now the caddy-masters' quarters at Real Golf
Club San Sebastián. These men have been
responsible for much of Spain's golfing success in
recent decades and perhaps the main reason
for the game's increasing popularity among
the locals.

Olivar de la Hinojosa

Olivar de la Hinojosa Golf Club, el Campo de las Naciones, 28042 Madrid
TEL: *917 21 18 89* **FAX:** *917 21 06 61*
LOCATION: *Close to Barajas Airport between the M40 and the N11 motorways, next to el Campo de las Naciones.*
COURSE: *18 holes, 6163m/6740yd, par 72, SSS 72*
GREEN FEES: *££*
FACILITIES: *Clubhouse, driving range, covered driving range, buggy hire, hand and electric trolley hire, pitching and putting green, practice bunker, golf tuition, club hire, pro-shop, restaurant, bar and showers.*

With Madrid nearby, this is a very popular course and you may find it difficult to get a tee time at Olivar – but it is possible. One of the few 'pay and play' type facilities near the city, the layout is not fantastic, but then any course will do for the golf-hungry visitor in a city that is not renowned for visitor-friendly golf!

Olivar is a medium-length tract with a fair sprinkling of trees, sand and water. Combined with generous fairways and more than the occasional rise it is not an easy proposition from the rear tees, but good golfers will enjoy the challenge. Less accurate players will enjoy it also, but more from the front tees. There is a double green for the 9th and 18th, which also share the borders of a large lake.

On the down side, the course does show signs of excessive traffic and more could be done to keep it in good order.

Castillo de Gorraiz

Castillo de Gorraiz Golf Club, Ctra. Huarte-Francia, 31620 Valle de Egues, Navarra
TEL: *948 33 70 73* **FAX:** *948 33 73 15*
LOCATION: *Just north of Pamplona in el Concejo de Olaz.*
COURSE: *18 holes, 6310m/6900yd, par 72, SSS 73*
GREEN FEES: *£££*
FACILITIES: *Clubhouse, covered driving range, buggy hire, free hand trolley, electric trolley hire, pitching and putting greens, practice bunker, golf tuition, club hire, pro-shop, restaurant, bar, changing rooms and showers.*

This course is set on a resort/sports complex, and it is well worth staying in this beautiful area for a few days. The facilities are varied and of the highest standards. They include tennis and swimming as well as an excellent golf course.

American designer Cabell B. Robinson was drafted in and, like his other projects such as La Cala in Southern Spain, he has done an admirable job.

There is plenty of room for every type of player here, but from the raised tees, the driver is not always the club of choice. As with La Cala North, it pays to play for position and not to get too near to the bunkers or the tangled rough. The greens are spacious and rolling, which means that this is a course of two games – first getting to the green in regulation and then putting it away. The second part could prove the more difficult.

Pamplona is a few kilometres south, and is worth a visit.

Above: A driver is not always the club of choice on the tees of Castillo de Gorraiz.

6 *Ulzama*

Ulzama Golf Club, Ctra. Francia, 31799 Navarra
TEL: *948 30 51 62* **FAX:** *948 30 54 71*
LOCATION: *From Iron take the N121A south towards Pamplona and then head towards el Valle de Ulzama.*
COURSE: *18 holes, 6232m/6815yd, par 72, SSS 72*
GREEN FEES: *£££*
FACILITIES: *Clubhouse, driving range, hand trolley hire, putting green, practice bunker, club hire, pro-shop, restaurant, bar and showers.*

Ulzama is quite an old club for this region. It opened as a nine-hole in 1965 and extended to 18 holes in 1990. Its location in el Valle de Ulzama is very much affected by the mountainous surroundings, and the course requires some stamina to get around.

The course is also influenced by the dense woods that it is cut through. Consequently, players must be able to aim the ball well, as the tree-lined fairways, while not tight, will not let off misdirected tee shots. A good drive is almost essential on many holes in order to have a chance at par.

With the course's up-and-down nature, most holes are evident from the tee and the hazards easily discernible. The greens are not complicated; they are generally flat with enough space. The back nine holes play the best, a rolling, rhythmic section that most players enjoy.

WINES OF NORTHERN SPAIN

Southwest of the town of Pamplona in the La Rioja region, the most famous of Spain's red wine, the Rioja, is produced. This most prestigious grape produces a lovely mellow wine, full-bodied with more than a touch of vanilla. Some of the most important *bodegas* in the region were founded by émigrés from the Bordeaux region in nearby France. They brought their expertise into this unique district, where the dry plains of Ebro meet the wetter, cooler hillsides of the Basque region. Distinct white and rosé wine also comes from the area using the Viura grape. Further east in Navarra, the region's reds, given a unique process, are not dissimilar in flavour to Rioja. Try a glass of Chivite to compare.

The Basque country is a little cool for wine production, but there are several small *bodegas* nonetheless. Galicia to the west is also cool and wet, yet it produces several local varieties such as Ribeiro, a slightly gassy table wine, Albarino, Loureira and Valdeorras.

Schedule lunch at one of the vineyards in the La Rioja valley, where you can sample a superb dish of lamb barbecued over the cuttings from last year's vines. And of course, wine tastes so much better when drunk on the land of its origin.

7 San Sebastián

*Real Golf Club de San Sebastián, Ctra. N1 Madrid–
Irun, Urb. Jaizkibel 20280 Hondarribia, Pais Vasco*
TEL: *943 61 68 45* **FAX:** *943 61 14 91*
LOCATION: *On A8 motorway , exit 4 towards Irun.*
COURSE: *18 holes, 5680m/6212yd, par 71, SSS 70*
GREEN FEES: *£££*
FACILITIES: *Clubhouse, covered driving range, hand
and electric trolley hire, pitching and putting greens,
practice bunker, club hire, caddy, pro-shop, restaurant,
bar, tennis court and showers.*

Golf star José María Olazábal grew up on
this property, and his present home is
the casa overlooking the 2nd fairway, which
makes San Sebastián a little more special. Oli
himself is often seen on the driving range.

It is obvious from the 1st hole that this is a
hilly course. Even the driving range is uphill,
which is very apt. The course is excellently set
up. It is short from the visitors' tees and if you
can play on sloping terrain you could score
well. Most tees are elevated, as are most of the
greens, and both call for a variety of shots. A
negative aspect is the number of tilting, usually
right to left, fairways. These can cause a good
drive to run off into semi-rough or worse.

*Above: Mist-shrouded hills form the backdrop to San
Sebastián golf course, a view enjoyed from the casa of the
Olazábal family.*

Other than that, the fairways are usually lush,
so they tend to slow and hold the ball. You
soon learn to be precise on these slanting holes.

The 1st plays downhill with a burn crossing
the fairway at around 230m/250yd then up to
an elevated green protected by bunkers left and
right. The hole is tree-lined all the way, but
this should not present problems. The 2nd is
wide and easier, although the sloping fairway
from right to left makes for difficulty. The large
green is divided into two distinct levels with
the break running front to back, so you want
to aim for the pin section.

The 3rd again offers a sloping fairway. Small
target greens are often approached from a
sideways or uphill lie. Blind tee shots are
common, but equally so are raised tees giving
clear views of the fairway. The 7th, perhaps the
most difficult, is a long par 4. The 16th and
17th are totally flat but well bunkered,
especially the 17th with three large bunkers
occluding the entrance to the green.

🏌 *Basozábal*

San Sebastián Basozábal Golf Club, Camino de
Goyaz-Txiki,41 (Caserio Goyaz Aundi) 20014,
San Sebastián
TEL: 943 46 76 42 **FAX:** 943 46 79 84
LOCATION: *Leaving San Sebastián, towards Hernani.
Follow the signs towards Oriamendi but keep your eyes
open – this is not an easy course to find.*
COURSE: *9 holes, 3073m/3360yd, par 72,*
GREEN FEES: *££££*
FACILITIES: *Clubhouse, covered driving range, hand
trolleys, pitching and putting greens, practice bunker,
pro-shop, restaurant, bar and showers.*

Local hero José María Olazábal is
personally involved with this project. He
has invested his time and expertise to help
create a course that will, no doubt, become
one of the best in the area. At present it is
only nine holes, but the degree of difficulty in
both the terrain and course's set-up makes for
a considerable challenge.

A combination of length and narrow
fairways on a terrain that is often sloping
takes its toll. You can see that
Olazábal would be comfortable
here as the terrain is not unlike
his home club of Real San
Sebastián. In such a
mountainous area it would
be difficult to build any
other kind of course.
Some water comes
into play at the 4th
and 6th.

The best approach
for all of the holes is
to play for position
and expect to bogey
each hole, otherwise
you are likely to drop
more shots than you care
to by making mistakes. This
is definitely a course on which
to develop your discipline.

MIGUEL ANGEL JIMENEZ

Miguel Angel Jímenez is one of Spain's most
admired golfers, and his qualities both on and off
the course have made him very popular. Jímenez
came from humble beginnings as an apprentice in
a garage in his home village of Churriana near
Málaga, next door to the Málaga Parador course
(see p.70). His older brother Juan encouraged and
taught him the game of golf and it was soon
apparent that he could be a gifted player. He
turned professional in 1982 and began his rise
through the ranks. Jímenez won the Turespaña
Open in 1999, along with the Volvo Masters, as
well as being part of the winning Spanish Team
at the Alfred Dunhill event in St Andrews. He
also made his Ryder Cup debut during that year,
then went on to tie for second place at the 2000
US Open at Pebble Beach.

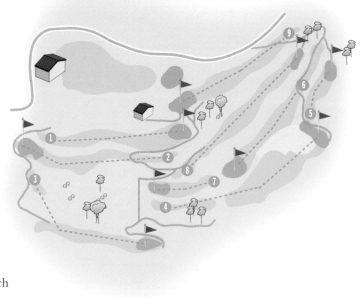

Neguri

Real Golf Club Neguri, Campo La Galea, Aptdo de Correos 9, E-48990 Algorta, Bilbao
TEL: *944 91 02 00* **FAX:** *944 60 56 11*
LOCATION: *From Bilbao Airport, motorway to Getxo then Algorta. Through town and ask directions as it is set in suburbs though not hard to find.*
COURSE: *18 holes, 6280m/6868yd, par 72, SSS 72*
GREEN FEES: *£££££*
FACILITIES: *Hand trolley hire, putting green, restaurant, bar, locker room and showers.*
VISITORS: *Visitors allowed weekdays only and handicap certificate is essential.*

Neguri sports a plaque awarding it the status of 'one of the finest golf courses in the world', but with indifferent greenkeeping and few services for visitors, it is hard to see why. This is very much a members' club. You need to produce your handicap certificate and have a tee time booked before you are admitted on to the property.

The 1st is a good opener, a drive and a 3-wood to a long, thin green with no real issue apart from the elongated bunker to the right of the green. The 3rd opens out to the sea and coastal breezes. There is trouble on the right,

so play left off the tee if you tend to fade. The fairways on the front half are wide and generous, but if you stray, mainly to the right, there is serious, ball-losing trouble. The greens are large and often elongated as at the 5th. If the pin is at the back it could leave a long putt of some 18m/20yd.

The 8th is a dogleg left, but the rough infringes on the right side. Go for sure placement here and it's an easy shot onto the green. The back nine kicks off with a long dogleg left with tall, elegant pine trees fringing both flanks. The tall pines dominate this section, which can make for difficult driving conditions. The 11th is another good dogleg right.

The 14th is a tough par 3 of 185m/200yd to an elevated green with a devastating bunker at the left foot. Into the wind it could be a 3-wood, but it might be more sensible to play with a mid-iron to the bunker and pitch on for a possible par-saving putt.

Below: Neguri's 10th is a tricky dogleg. The back nine of this course is more tree-lined.

 **Laukariz**

*Laukariz Golf Club, Ctra. Bibao–Bermeo, Urb. Monte
Berreaga 48100, Pais Vasco*
TEL: *946 74 08 58* **FAX:** *946 74 08 62*
LOCATION: *On the road Bilbao–Bermeo, before getting
to Mungia. Turn right, towards Laukariz.*
COURSE: *18 holes, 6481m/7087yd, par 72, SSS 72*
GREEN FEES: *£££*
FACILITIES: *Clubhouse, driving range, covered driving
range, hand trolley hire, pitching and putting greens,
practice bunker, golf tuition, club hire and repair, pro-
shop, restaurant, bar and showers.*

Laukariz is a popular course. It is the only alternative to Neguri for golf in the Bilbao area, and Neguri is a private course that will admit visitors but only at a premium green fee. This means that Laukariz tends to get crowded at peak times with both local players and members jostling for tees.

The course is quite challenging. It is set in part in a valley and a lot of consideration is required for many of the tight and testing holes. Thick vegetation tends to narrow the fairways with water making an appearance on holes such as the 11th. The course is certainly friendly and open to visitors, but you must book in advance or choose a quiet time of day.

 **Matalenas**

*Matalenas Golf Club, Ctra. del Faro s/n, 39080
Santander, Cantabria*
TEL: *942 39 02 47* **FAX:** *942 39 02 47*
LOCATION: *From Santander take the road towards the
lighthouse and to El Sardinero Avenue.*
COURSE: *9 holes, 4576m/5004yd, par 68,
SSS 66*
GREEN FEES: *££*
FACILITIES: *Clubhouse, driving range, hand trolley
hire, pitching and putting greens, practice bunker, golf
tuition, club hire, restaurant, bar and showers.*

This is a short nine-holer playing away from the clubhouse out on to a thin peninsula. The views in every direction are stunning, with shipping passing out into the Bay of Biscay. The 4th stands out at the peninsula's tip, a par 3 that is slightly sheltered by trees to the north but usually catching any breezes to make it longer than assumed. Coming back in are views over to the cliffs and beach or Playa de Matalenas, with a stone wall to stop golfers from straying too close to the edge. This is a fun course, most refreshing and definitely worth sampling if you are staying in this area or even if you are disembarking from the ferry.

THE GUGGENHEIM MUSEUM

If there was a singular example of how one piece of extraordinary architecture could turn an old industrial port into a top tourist destination it is the Guggenheim Museum in Bilbao. Opened in 1997, the 'Gugg' has become a major tourist attraction. Tour buses disgorge thousands of visitors every day of the year (except on Mondays when the museum is closed).

Designed by Frank O. Gehry and resembling a giant titanium armadillo, the museum is dedicated to 20th-century American and European art. The building is a superb feat of engineering and architecture, featuring orthogonal blocks of limestone, glass walls and titanium panels. The building is made up of interconnected blocks with some 29 galleries, an auditorium, a restaurant and shop.

The museum is the sister gallery of the Guggenheim museums in Venice and New York. The Bilbao gallery focuses on Spanish luminaries such as Picasso, Chillida, Miro and Tapies. It also carries works by internationally renowned modern artists such as Yves Klein, Willem de Kooning, Andy Warhol and Jean-Michel Basquiat. The museum also shows work by leading contemporary Basque and Spanish artists.

THE PILGRIM ROUTE

El Camino de Santiago – the Way of Saint James or the Pilgrim Route – takes various roads through France and Northern Spain all the way to the religious city of Santiago de Compostela, one of Galicia's few major population centres. The route follows the legendary journey of Saint James who, it is claimed, came to Spain not long after the crucifixion of Christ to spread the gospel, and whose body was returned there after his death.

The pilgrimage became popular after the discovery of Saint James's body in the 9th century, and villages, hospices and monasteries sprung up all along the thousand-mile route. In medieval times this would have been an arduous and extremely adventurous trip to make, but is was considered worth it by the many who believed in the miracles of Saint James, who allegedly had the power to reduce pilgrims' time spent in purgatory. The route soon became fashionable and the pilgrims were joined by people trying to widen their horizons.

As early as the 12th century a guidebook to the route was available and Santiago de Compostela is widely considered to be Europe's first tourist destination. Although El Camino de Santiago is still popular today, it is likely that the majority of those who choose to commit themselves to the long-distance walk, or even a mere section of it, undertake it for the glory of the beautiful countryside and culture to be found en route rather than for the remission of their sins.

12 *Abra del Pas*

Abra del Pas Golf Club, Ctra. del Camping de Mogro, 39310 Cantabria
TEL: *942 57 75 97*
LOCATION: *15km from Santander and 8km from Torrelavega on the Camping de Mogro road.*
COURSE: *9 holes, 6158m/6734yd, par 72, SSS 72*
GREEN FEES: *££*
FACILITIES: *Clubhouse, driving range, hand trolley hire, putting green, practice bunker, golf tuition, club hire, club repair, bar and showers.*

Although only a nine-hole course, it is well worth making an excursion to Abra del Pas Golf Club.

Set on the mouth of the River Abra del Pas, it occupies a quiet spot away from busy Santander. It has a lovely peaceful location with trees, dunes and plenty of sandy bunkers defining the course. It is not a short course either, with several lengthy par 4s that call for accurate drives and long and sometimes lucky approach shots to clear the trees or waiting bunkers on to the greens.

13 *De Lugo*

De Lugo Golf Club, Ctra. Portomarin 27188, Santa Marta de Fixos, Galicia
TEL: *982 17 63 14*
LOCATION: *Road to Portomarín. Turn for Terlama and signposted.*
COURSE: *9 holes, 6012m/6575yd, par 72, SSS 72*
GREEN FEES: *£*
FACILITIES: *Clubhouse, covered driving range, free hand trolley, pitching and putting greens, practice bunker, golf tuition, club hire, club repair, bar and showers.*

De Lugo is a pleasant nine-hole layout, long where it needs to be with plenty of landing room. A driver can be used to good effect, setting up opportunities for a low score. However, de Lugo is not a pushover and water hazards, mainly two lakes, a small stream and larger river, take their toll. Trees are also a feature of this wonderfully landscaped area and good golfers will come off here both enamoured at the course's setting and perhaps amused at how testing it is.

14 La Coruña

Club de Golf de La Coruña, La Zapateira, Zapateira s/n, 15191 La Coruña
TEL: *981 28 52 00* FAX: *981 28 03 32*
LOCATION: *7km from La Coruña, in the mountain area of La Zapateira.*
COURSE: *18 holes*
GREEN FEES: *££ (working days) ££££ (weekends and Bank holidays)*
FACILITIES: *Clubhouse, covered driving range, free hand trolley, putting green, golf tuition, club hire, club repair, restaurant, bar, fitness centre, sauna and showers.*

Opened in 1962 and designed by Mackenzie Ross, La Coruña is a private club set in a wonderful mountainous location. Visitors are allowed to play, but you must arrange times in advance to fit with the club's available times.

The course is relatively hazardous due to its pine wood and mountain setting. There are a number of interesting holes. The 4th is a long par 4 of 459m/502yd and unshakeably difficult. The main trouble, besides the length of the fairway, is its narrowness and a steep rise to the right. Another long and challenging hole is the 6th, a par 5 at 536m/586yd, with a dogleg to the left.

The fairway is more accommodating than the 'wasp-waist' 4th, but a lake borders the green on the left and it is particularly well bunkered. Unless you achieve a perfect position off the tee and strike a strong 3-wood up the middle, you will find it difficult to find the ideal wedge-shot position into the green.

The 10th is a magnificent par 4 with, again, a narrow fairway surrounded by pines rising gently towards the green. To finish, the 16th is a very difficult par 4. The first stroke is blind over a hill and even from the second shot there is a very poor view of the green. The second stroke is further complicated by the river that crosses the fairway.

15 Club de Santiago

Real Aero Club de Santiago, Labacolla, 15701 Santiago de Compostela, Galicia
TEL: *981 59 24 00*
FAX: *981 59 24 00*
LOCATION: *Located next to Santiago de Compostela airport.*
COURSE: *9 holes, 5622m/6148yd, par 70, SSS 69*
GREEN FEES: *£*
FACILITIES: *Clubhouse, covered driving range, free hand trolley, putting green, golf tuition, club hire, club repair, restaurant, bar, fitness centre, sauna and showers.*

Santiago's course is quite flat and fairly short, but its nine small greens and varying tee positions make it quite challenging. Trees are the main ingredient in a round here and you will do well not to tangle with them although it is probably inevitable at some stage during your round. Water also comes into play, in the form of two lakes.

The 20-year-old course has relatively short and tight fairways. The accurate, steady player will love the many trees, especially pine, which surround the course demanding precise tee shots. These create an excellent challenge where straight, positional play comes into its own.

The more wayward striker might come off this course slightly frustrated, though. If your driver is not behaving you should consider leaving it in the car. The greens tend to be small and well protected, so the need for accuracy never stops on a round at Santiago.

While the course is not particularly lengthy, most players find that they sacrifice length for position and so do not find the greens in regulation.

There are some water hazards to look out for on the course, but most players will remember the tight fairways as the course's main defence.

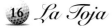

La Toja

La Toja Golf Club, Isla de la Toja, Ria de Arosa, 36991 Galicia
TEL: 986 73 32 32 **FAX:** 986 73 31 22
WWW: www.latojagolf.com
EMAIL: infor@ latojagolf.com
LOCATION: Located on the little island of La Toja, 70km from Santiago de Compostela and 65km from Vigo.
COURSE: 9 holes, 5938m/6494yd, par 72, SSS 72
GREEN FEES: ££££
FACILITIES: Clubhouse, driving range, covered driving range, buggy hire, hand trolley hire, pitching and putting greens, practice bunker, golf tuition, club hire, pro-shop, restaurant, bar, swimming pool and showers.
VISITORS: Open to members, visitors staying at la Isla de La Toja, and hotel residents.

Situated in the heart of Galicia, La Toja is about as tight a course as you could want. Opened in 1970, it is set on an island-like peninsula with water affecting five of the nine holes and thick pine woods defining the rest. It is an accurate player's delight and a sprayer's dismay. Steady progress will be made with a long iron.

La Toja is an island of 96 hectares. On this islet skirted by the beaches of the Ria de Arosa, there are effectively 18 holes with two sets of tees on all but the 3rd and 6th. Players seem delighted to take on the same hole from a slightly different angle or length. The 3rd is a par 5, 504m/551yd. The green and the river can be seen

Above: Set on a peninsula, La Toja's holes are often affected by water.

from the top of the sloping tee position. The green is open with gentle slopes that are not always easy to read. Precision is needed on the 4th, where there is a long carry off the tee over water with strategically placed bunkers waiting to catch the drive. The 5th green teeters on the edge of the sea and, although short (par 3 of 120m/130yd), can be lengthened by the wind. The 17th is narrow with rough on the left and the sea on the right. This combination of tight tee shots, target approaches and a relatively flat terrain makes La Toja an exciting yet easy walking venue.

Ria de Vigo

Ria de Vigo, San Lorenzo-Domaio, Moaña, 36950 Pontevedra
TEL: 986 32 70 51 **FAX:** 986 32 70 53
WWW: riadevigogolf.com
E-MAIL: riadevigogolf@riadevigogolf.com
LOCATION: On the Morrazo peninsula, about 15km from Vigo city.
COURSE: 18 holes, 6110m/6682yd, par 72, SSS 72
FACILITIES: Clubhouse, covered driving range, hand trolley hire, putting green, golf tuition, club repair, pro-shop, restaurant, bar, children's playground, swimming pool, tennis court and showers.

Opened in 1992, Ria de Vigo is a relatively hazardous mountain course with splendid views across the river and Vigo city. The course is set in an incomparable landscape. Its 18 holes mix difficulty, beauty and quality. Its many lakes and water hazards are due to the River Muiño. The water hazards are spread all along the course and make you pay attention to every stroke. From the elevated tee of the 4th there is a magnificent view of the river. The drive drops steeply onto a narrow fairway with a boundary to the right and a slope with thick rough on the left. The second shot is usually short back onto an elevated green. The 5th, par 4, has a hill going up towards the green. The river divides the fairway so players have to choose between two different courses.

The short 7th is a straightforward hole once you know it, but first-timers might fall foul of the large lake that cannot be seen from the tee. The river also divides the fairway on the 12th hole, offering two ways to play it. To the left the hole is shorter but it is possible to miss the fairway and get lost in rough. The hole plays longer to the right but is less complicated despite the river crossing the front of the green.

18 Club de Vigo

Real Aero Club de Vigo, Reconquista 7, 36201 Vigo, Galicia
TEL: *986 48 66 45* **FAX:** *986 48 66 43*
LOCATION: *8km from Vigo, near the airport.*
COURSE: *9 holes, 5622m/6148yd, par 70, SSS 69*
GREEN FEES: *££*
FACILITIES: *Clubhouse, covered driving range, hand trolley hire, putting green, golf tuition, club repair, pro-shop, restaurant, bar, children's playground, swimming pool, tennis court and showers.*

Club de Vigo is another nine-hole course that is demanding of accuracy and good strategic play. Trees, water and out-of-bounds are the three ingredients that put the screws on Vigo's course. Length is also required from time to time, so all elements of your game will be tested here.

The fun starts right at the 1st, where absolute perfection is called for to carry a lake. Many players find it a little too demanding if they are at all rusty. If there is a case for spending time on a practice range before coming onto a course, this is it. The 6th hole might appear quite easy, but many find the bunkers, especially on the right.

19 Mondariz

Campo de Golf de Mondariz, Mondariz-Balneario Pontevedra, 36890 Pontevedra
TEL: *986 62 62 00* **FAX:** *986 66 45 12*
E-MAIL: *golfmondariz@infonegocio.com*
LOCATION: *In the spa town of Mondariz, situated inland 30km from Vigo on the Madrid road at the Puenteareas turn-off.*
COURSE: *18 holes, 5790m/6332yd, Par 71*
GREEN FEES: *£*
FACILITIES: *Clubhouse, changing room and showers, driving range, buggy hire, hand and electric trolley hire, pitching and putting greens, practice bunker, golf tuition, club repair, club rental, pro-shop, hotel, restaurant, bar, children's playground.*

This is an inland, gently sloping course, with several holes bordered by the River Tea. Most holes have more than one tee and offer a choice of play. Wide, sloping greens with a variety of flag positions create various possibilities for playing the holes.

The course's first real test comes at the 10th, a par 4 of 300m/328yd with a spectacular green surrounded by bunkers offering several levels of difficulty depending upon the different flag positions. The course's signature hole occurs at the 17th, a par 3 of 200m/219yd. With a lake to the right and a bunker on the opposite side, it is a daunting proposition. However, the 18th is easier; it is a wide par 5 with lots of room to turn the shoulders. It is a dogleg to the left and finishes with a large green.

ENTERTAINMENT IN GALICIA

There are a multitude of little restaurants specializing in fish and seafood along the Atlantic coast of Galicia. The famous Fiesta del Marsico is celebrated every year during the week of the 12th October. The area is an important tourist destination famous for its hotels, casino, water sports and the hot baths at Ria de Arosa.

REGIONAL DIRECTORY

Where to stay – Central Spain

In the southwest near Badajoz is the **Confortel Badajoz** (924 44 37 11) next door to Guadiana golf course, as well as the **Hotel Zurbarán** in downtown Badajoz.

In Madrid there is a fair chance you will visit this city for reasons other than golf – either business or sightseeing. A hotel in town ideally placed for exploring the city is the **Hotel Emperador** in Old Madrid (915 47 28 00). In spite of its proximity to the traffic, it is surprisingly quiet, and offers the attraction of a roof-top swimming pool. If you want to put on the style, try **The Ritz** (915 21 28 57), one of Madrid's most graceful hotels.

Where to eat – Central Spain

Extremadura is renowned for its hearty roast meals. Try the best restaurants in Badajoz, **El Sotano** (924 44 82 96) or **Aldebarán** (924 27 42 61). In Madrid you must go to the **Botín** in Old Madrid (913 66 42 17). It is reputed to date back to 1725 and the traditional Castilian roast lamb and suckling pig are fantastic. Another exquisite Madrid eatery is **El Amparo** (914 31 64 56).

Where to go – Central Spain

Extremadura is know for its Roman ruins, while Madrid is famous for its architecture and museums. The **Plaza Mayor** (Main Square) is worth a stroll around, and the **Centro de Arte Reina Sofía** is a modern art museum well worth visiting. Madrid is all about nightlife, though, and you cannot go far wrong if you are looking for an exciting evening. **Plaza de Santa Ana** is the place to head for beginners, with cafes and clubs open until the early hours of the morning. Hemingway used to hang out here. Beware – it can be expensive, especially the tapas. The bars themselves are interesting tourist sights. There is so much to see and do in Madrid but not a lot of golf – so why are you here?

Where to stay – Northern Spain

Bilbao is an up-and-coming tourist destination. If you want to stay here then the town centre is best. The **Hotel Carlton** is right in the middle (944 16 22 00) but its five-star status is a little questionable. Alternatively in Algora, closer to Neguri Golf Club, there is the **Hotel Igeretxe** (944 91 00 09) overlooking the beach. Here the sights and sounds are a lot more laid back apart from the industrial landscape on the other side of the harbour. If you are visiting Pedrena to play Seve's home course, the accommodation is not great in town nor in the adjacent conurbation. Play the course and carry on into Santander to stay at the **Real** (942 27 25 50). This is near the Playa de la Magdelena and offers a bit of class. There are also plenty of hotels along these beach areas.

Carrying on west, the roads become a little trying after Santander. Most visitors to Galicia are probably better off flying directly into Santiago.

Where to eat – Northern Spain

Bilbao is awash with excellent little restaurants – so don't eat in the hotels – go out and explore for yourself. Highly recommended is **Restaurante Guria** (944 41 57 80) on the Gran Vía, a few minutes walk from the city centre. There is an upmarket tapas bar to the front and a very elegant small restaurant to the rear – expensive and slightly fussy. Otherwise roam and try whatever takes your fancy – you will not go wrong in any of the proper restaurants (not the snack bars or downmarket cafes). Galicia has perhaps the best seafood in Spain. In Pontevedra try the elegant **Casa Solla** (986 87 28 84) for some of the best preparations. **El Castillo** in Vigo (986 42 11 11) offers stunning views from its hilltop situation.

Where to go – Northern Spain

San Sebastián is an elegant holiday resort and is ideally situated to explore the interior as well as southwest France and **Biarritz**, a good golfing area. In July, head inland to **Pamplona** for its annual fiesta 'Los Sanfermines'. You have probably seen or heard about the bull stampede called 'the Encierro' where mad young men run ahead of the bulls – don't get in the way but enjoy the spectacle from the sidelines.

Below: Bilbao's Guggenheim Museum gives way to some extraordinary exhibitions.

Chapter 6

The Balearic Islands

The Balearic Islands lie 240km (150 miles) from the Spanish mainland. The smaller islands of Menorca and Ibiza (respectively northeast and southwest of the main island of Mallorca) each offer a nine-hole golf course, but generally they are the domain of other types of tourism. Menorca is relaxed, quiet and ideal for family holidays, while Ibiza has become Europe's biggest centre of dance culture and clubbing.

The large island of Mallorca attracts a remarkable diversity of visitors. The island is a holiday haven for the very wealthy and glamorous such as Hollywood stars Elizabeth Taylor, Michael Douglas and model Claudia Schiffer. Members of the Spanish Royal family play golf here, and Saudi Arabian princes own acres of prime property. Mallorca also is the number one

Left: Bendinat offers a tight driving proposition at the 14th. Above: Palma cathedral is probably the city's most popular tourist attraction.

destination for package holidaymakers from Northern Europe. They mainly gather around the towns of Magalluf, Palmanova and Cala Rajada. Fortunately the island is large enough to accommodate everyone, and there are still many unique and unexpected aspects of Spanish culture to be discovered.

Golfing on the Balearics

As a golf destination, the main island of Mallorca is most prominent. Golf has had a presence on the island since 1964 with the opening of Son Vida Golf Club just outside Palma. Currently golfers can choose from 15 courses and a further five are under development. Mallorca continues to grow in the quantity and variety of golf that it offers.

The main city of Palma is a useful base for a golfing trip. From here it takes only minutes by *autopista* to access the courses of the southwest such as Santa Ponsa, Bendinat or Poniente. You can also reach the courses in and around Palma, whereas

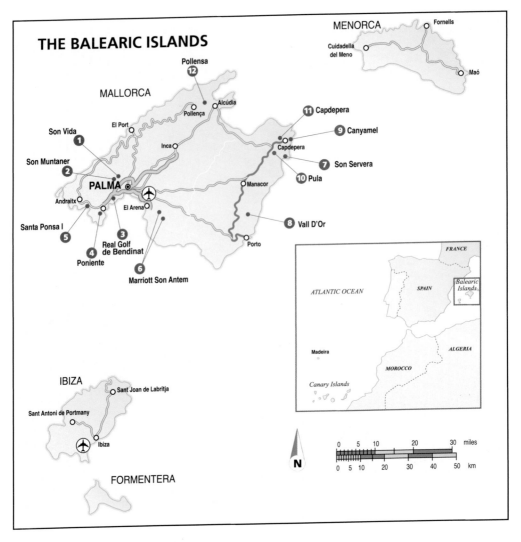

it takes at least an hour to drive to the courses in the northeast. The ideal arrangement for golfers might therefore be to book a two-centre holiday and spend a few days in each of these well-provided areas.

As with other southern Spanish destinations, the high season for golf in the Balearics is through the winter months. Courses become busier from October and peak in popularity around Christmas. From February until April is also a popular time. Generally green fees are more expensive in the Balearics than on mainland Spain, being around £35 or more. Golf in the summer months is feasible early or late in the day with a cart. You will find the courses in good condition and very quiet at this time.

Golfers coming from well-maintained Northern European or American courses might find the standards of greenkeeping a little lacking in the Balearics, especially on some of the older courses. Bear in mind that this is due to dry, hot weather through much of the year. The newer courses seem to have set a higher standard of maintenance and are overcoming irrigation and agronomy problems to present excellent playing conditions.

Besides golf, there are plenty of other activities and attractions throughout the islands. Water sports and sailing are popular, with a host of marinas dotted around the coast. Traditional beach holidays are still very popular. There are many lovely sandy coves and welcomingly warm weather from spring to autumn. The island is popular with tourists – some 800 plane-loads of holidaymakers can land at Palma de Mallorca Airport on a busy day – but it is amazing how quiet and secluded the island can be if you avoid the obvious tourist spots.

Palma has several good courses with excellent accommodation throughout the city. If you want to explore the city as well as the area's courses, the most noteworthy buildings in Palma are the cathedral and the 14th-century castle, which offers unrivalled views across the city. As in every other part of Spain, evenings revolve around eating and drinking. Burgers and chips are available for the unadventurous, but Mallorcan cooking is good and plentiful and definitely worth exploring.

Magalluf and Palmanova are Mallorca's package-holiday resorts. There is plenty of golf nearby, but the general hubbub of these resorts might not suit the golfing mentality. Golfers seeking good standards of accommodation with excellent restaurants nearby should seek out Portals Nous, Santa Ponsa or go further west to Cap de Mar. At the opposite end of the island, Cala Rajada is popular, especially with German tourists, but it can be rather gregarious especially at night. There are many other cove communities along the east coast worth seeking out.

Accommodation-wise, there are many *Fincas* or converted farmhouses available as an alternative to hotels. These are usually in a country setting with a relaxed atmosphere and good, private amenities. For a small group of holiday-makers, *Fincas* can prove most economical as well as being very pleasant. More information about these can be found at www.toptravel.com.

Getting around

Mallorca is well served with an *autopista* system stretching from the airport west to Palmanova. The vía Cintura is part of the same route skirting to the north of Palma. It is as quick, less frenetic and more scenically interesting to travel across Palma via the port.

Driving in the Balearics presents little problem. You can also use taxis at a reasonable cost; 2000 pesetas (£10) would take you one-way from Palma to Santa Ponsa. Some hotels offer shuttle services to the golf courses.

If you decide to travel to the other Balearic islands of Menorca, Ibiza or Formentera, the best option is to use inter-island planes. Try to book well in advance if possible as seats are usually at a premium.

Golf handicaps

As throughout most of Spain, official golf handicaps are necessary. Some clubs will not ask for them but most do, so do not leave home without one. They may also ask for a golfing 'green card'. These are a peculiarity of European countries although not used in the UK or North America. If you do not have one, golfing officials will usually understand why when you explain where you are from.

 ## Son Vida

Son Vida Golf Club, Urb. Son Vida, 07013 Palma de Mallorca, Mallorca
TEL: *971 79 12 10* **FAX:** *971 79 11 27*
EMAIL: *sonvidagolf@readysoft.es*
LOCATION: *Take the vía Cintura and exit north for Son Rapina and continue 1.5km. The course is well signposted but do not confuse for Son Vida Hotel off to the right.*
COURSE: *18 holes, 5740m/6277yd, par 72, SSS 71*
GREEN FEES: *££££*
FACILITIES: *Clubhouse, driving range, covered driving range, buggy hire, hand trolley hire, pitching and putting greens, practice bunker, golf tuition, club hire, pro-shop, restaurant, bar and snacks, changing rooms and showers.*

Above: Many of the holes at San Vida golf course play through shady avenues. The course is very near Palma, but its fairways offer a quiet retreat from the busy city.

Son Vida was the first and, for a long time, the only golf course on Mallorca. It is a little tired now, but restoration is under way. The course is only minutes from busy Palma so it is a pleasure to wander through its secluded, leafy avenues in relative quiet. The front nine tends to be narrow and tree-lined, whereas the second nine is more open. It is not a long course but it does demand accuracy especially from the back tees – visitors are free to use these. This makes the course all the more enjoyable; from these tees, taking on the numerous doglegs is not such a straightforward task for low handicappers. The greens are not too big either, so a good game can be had by working on accuracy rather than distance.

The 3rd is a trying uphill par 4 and turns on the test. The 11th is a par 5, long and also uphill demanding two firm strikes to gain an attacking position at the elevated green. The 16th is also notable, a challenging par 3 from a series of elevated tees with three large bunkers and a small pond surrounding this compact green. Finally, the 18th is a challenging dogleg to round off a surprisingly stimulating little layout.

2 Son Muntaner

*Son Muntaner Golf Club, Urb. Son Vida, 07013
Palma de Mallorca*
TEL: *971 79 12 10* **FAX:** *971 79 11 27*
EMAIL: *sonvidagolf@readysoft.es*
LOCATION: *Take the vía Cintura and exit north for
Son Rapina continuing for 1km. The course entrance is
on the left.*
COURSE: *18 holes, 6347m/6941yd, par 72, SSS 73*
GREEN FEES: *££££+*
FACILITIES: *Clubhouse, driving range, covered driving
range, buggy hire, hand trolley hire, pitching and putting
greens, practice bunker, golf tuition, club hire, pro-shop,
restaurant, bar and snacks, changing rooms and showers.*
VISITORS: *This course is exclusively for Arabella
Sherton and Son Vida guests and a handicap certificate is
required.*

This is a modern design with prominent mounding along the fairways and a distinct, flowing definition reminiscent of a Japanese garden. There is little heavy rough and just enough trees in play, so a game is never tedious, although bunkers are strategically placed. Tees are mainly raised so it is a pleasure to pick your spot for the drive.

The 1st is a tough opener. Out of bounds lines the right side of a stiff right dogleg and it is not unusual to start with 5 off the tee. Take an iron and play safely left to give a good approach position into the green which is also tucked hard into the right. The 2nd, a par 5, presents a daunting outlook with a bifurcated tree trunk blocking the fairway and some water to carry; well right of the tree is the best line.

The first four holes give the impression that this might be a difficult course. The key is to play safely through here and wait on the course to open as it does by the 6th. Here you play from on high down to a reasonable fairway with a wide lake on the right.

The 13th is deceptive, a short par 3 with a green that tails away, so be careful with club selection. Playing too short might catch the bunker that runs on the right side of the green.

There is no water on the back nine. The 15th is a tough par 5 dogleg right. If you take too much of the right corner and end up in the rough all is not lost as this is the direct line playing over the 16th tee. Note the ancient olive tree on this hole surrounded by a small stone wall.

*Below: Son Muntaner is one of the most pleasurable of
Mallorca's many good courses. You must stay at the
Arabella Sheraton or Hotel Son Vida to play the course.*

Real Golf de Bendinat

Real Golf de Bendinat, Illetas, Bendinat, Mallorca
TEL: *971 40 52 00* **FAX:** *971 70 07 86*
LOCATION: *7km from Palma; exit for Portals Nous and turn back towards Illetas. The entrance is clearly marked on the left.*
COURSE: *18 holes, 5650m/6179yd, par 70, SSS 71*
GREEN FEES: *££££*
FACILITIES: *Clubhouse, driving range, buggy hire, hand trolley hire, pitching and putting greens, practice bunker, golf tuition, club hire, pro-shop, restaurant, bar, changing rooms and showers.*

Bendinat is a hilly course, so a buggy is recommended. Elevated greens or tees are its hallmark. They have been laid out to provide inspiring views of Palma and the sea. Although by no means long, this is an interesting course and ideal for the club golfer's game.

The back nine has some lovely views over the island. The section from the 12th to the 15th is most notable. The 12th is a par 3 with a lake on the left. This is around a 7-iron distance; for safety, play to the right of green to avoid the water. At 294m (320yd) from the visitors' tee, the 13th is an excellent par 4. Although not long, it is very narrow off the tee and indeed all the way to the green. The 14th is a par 5 dogleg to the right with a castle view.

The club also produces a course guide that offers information on the local flora and fauna as well as golf. The striped Hoopoe and other interesting birds are to be spotted on the course. The club's conservation policies have led to recognition from the Audubon Society.

Poniente

Poniente Golf Club, Ctra. Cala Figuera s/n, 07182 Magalluf, Mallorca
TEL: *971 13 00 59* **FAX:** *971 13 01 76*
EMAIL: *poniente@futurnet.es*
LOCATION: *Follow the motorway west from Palma (15km) towards Andratx and exit at roundabout for Magalluf and El Toro.*
COURSE: *18 holes, 6140m/6715yd, par 72, SSS 72*
GREEN FEES: *££££*
FACILITIES: *Clubhouse, driving range, buggy hire, hand trolley hire, pitching and putting greens, practice bunker, golf tuition, club hire, pro-shop, restaurant, bar, changing rooms and showers.*

Poniente Golf Club is one of Mallorca's older courses, located just west of Magalluf. The clubhouse is striking – a pleasant terracotta-coloured building covered in bougainvillea. Chickens run freely around the clubhouse as well as the adjacent tees.

The course is in good condition and offers a varied and enjoyable, if occasionally hilly, test. The first holes play over a level valley and cross the road on several occasions. The 4th approaches the trees while the 5th doglegs right with huge waste bunkers left of the green. Playing back down to the level at the 10th, this tight dogleg has water at the corner and again right of the green and is probably the course's stiffest test.

The 16th offers a difficult driving proposition uphill, but you have the pleasure of playing downhill for the 17th and 18th. Most players will come off here with a sense of approval and achievement.

Above: The 17th and 18th holes at Poniente golf club play downhill, which is a welcome change from the uphill 16th, though generally the course is not difficult to walk.

Santa Ponsa I

Santa Ponsa Golf Club I, Urb. Santa Ponsa, 07180
Mallorca
TEL: 971 69 02 11 **FAX:** 971 69 33 64
LOCATION: *Exit for Santa Ponsa off the Motorway
Palma–Andratx, 18km from Palma and left at
roundabout. Keep going as there are several entrances that
are not the golf club.*
COURSE: *18 holes, 6543m/7155yd, par 72, SSS 72*
GREEN FEES: *££££+*
FACILITIES: *Clubhouse, driving range, covered driving
range, buggy hire, hand and electric trolley hire, 2 putting
greens, practice bunker, golf tuition, club hire, pro-shop,
restaurant in hotel, bar and snacks, changing rooms
and showers.*
VISITORS: *Players without official handicaps not
admitted.*

*Above: There are many hidden hazards to trick the
unwary golfer at Santa Ponsa I. Santa Ponsa II
and III are generally not available to visitors.*

Low handicap players will enjoy this
lengthy test, but mid to high handicaps
might find it a little too stretching.

The course looks innocuous from the tees
but few will play to their handicap, especially
on the first outing. There are many hidden
dangers, so either play once for orientation or
study the course plan closely. The 1st is a slight
dogleg and an easy if lengthy opener. This par
5 dogleg right invites you to take on the corner
but it is better to keep left taking a line just
inside the bunker. The 6th hides a deep creek
running across the approach. The 7th is a well-
protected par 3 tightened by the thick canopy
of trees on either side and a convoluted pond
system completely out of sight of the tee. The
8th green is set on an awkward mound with
bunkering either side, so a strong drive will
make the approach easier.

The back nine opens with a killer par 5.
Even without wind two good strikes will leave
a small green fronted by a huge waste of sand
to deal with. The 16th is a long par 4 with a
severe dogleg right. Do not by any means
block yourself out here by going at the right
corner. Play well left and avoid the trees to the
right. The approach is over water so play for
bogey and lay up or you will count the costs.

6 Marriott Son Antem

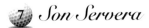

*Marriott Son Antem Golf Resort and Spa, 07602
Llucmajor, Mallorca*
TEL: *971 12 91 00* **FAX:** *971 12 91 01*
LOCATION: *From Palma past airport towards
Llucmajor around 18km. The resort is well signposted to
the right.*
COURSE: *East: 18 holes, 6325m/6917yd, par 72,
SSS 72; West: 18 holes, 6542m/7154yd, par 72,
SSS 72 (Open Oct 2001)*
GREEN FEES: *££££+*
FACILITIES: *Clubhouse, spa, golf academy, driving
range, buggy hire, trolley hire, pitching and putting
greens, practice bunkers, club hire, pro-shop, restaurant in
hotel, bar and snacks.*

Son Antem is the first resort project built
by US-based Marriott in Europe, so it
seems destined for great things. At the
moment, the existing East Course is fairly flat
and not too demanding, but is a pleasant
outing nonetheless. It is occasionally tight off
the tee: for instance, at the 7th, pine trees
leave only about 25-metre gap to drive
through. This long par 5 of 526m/575yd
will be difficult if you do not get the ball
away well.

The 11th is a
dogleg right, which
is easiest tackled
by playing left,
otherwise you will
be blocked out by
trees. The 12th is a
similar configuration
but beware of the
pond to the left of
the green, which is
out of sight until
you reach it.

The new West
Course will open
shortly to championship standard and with the
investment already made in design and
maintenance this will probably set new
standards in the Balearics. A circular practice

*Above: The existing East Course will soon be joined by
the Championship West Course.*

area is also being developed, offering every
possible on-course scenario. Plans for a golf
academy are equally appealing.

7 Son Servera

*Son Servera Golf Club, Urb. Costa de los Pinos,
07559 Son Servera, Mallorca*
TEL: *971 84 00 96* **FAX:** *971 84 01 60*
WWW: *golfsonserva.com*
EMAIL: *cgss@calamillor.com*
LOCATION: *Take the C715 road Palma–Manacor,
then turn right at Sant Llorenc towards Son Servera.
Head towards Costa de los Pinos, then turn left at
'Club de Golf'.*
COURSE: *9 holes, 5956m/6513yd, par 72,
SSS 72*
GREEN FEES: *£££*
FACILITIES: *Clubhouse, driving range, buggy
hire, hand trolley hire, putting green, practice
bunker, golf tuition, club repair, club hire,
pro-shop, restaurant, bar, changing rooms and
showers.*

Son Servera is one of the earlier golf
courses established on the island. It is
situated on the northeast coast in La Costa de
Los Pinos. Designed
by John Harris in
1967, the course is
rather narrow and
provides a moderate
challenge. With the
seashore nearby,
the course offers
some varied terrain,
playing through
a pine forest over
undulating land
with water coming
into play on the
final hole.

The course is an ideal length for a
casual game, but also has enough surprises
to keep most club golfers entertained
and challenged.

8 Vall D'Or

Vall D'Or Golf Club, Ctra. Porto Colom a Cala D'Or km7.7 07669 S'Horta, Mallorca
TEL: 971 83 70 01 **FAX:** 971 83 72 99
LOCATION: *Take the road from Porto Colom to Cala D'Or. The course is 8km from Porto Colom.*
COURSE: *18 holes, 5575m/6097yd, par 71, SSS 71*
GREEN FEES: £££
FACILITIES: *Clubhouse, driving range, covered driving range, buggy hire, hand trolley hire, pitching and putting greens, practice bunker, golf tuition, club repair, club hire, pro-shop, restaurant, bar and snacks, changing rooms and showers.*

Vall D'Or is set on the east side of the island about an hour's drive from the centre of Palma. It is not quite on the coast but there are sea views from many of its tree-lined holes. Gentle rises are the order of the day with plenty of room off the tee apart from one or two occasions when the woods almost encroach onto the greens. There are also narrow valleys where the fairways are forced to come in, leaving little room between the scrub-covered mounds.

The original nine holes set out in the mid-1980s are the most exciting. The rise and fall of the terrain, along with the many trees that line the fairways, makes for some good and testing play. The back nine includes a few uphill drives, which are always more demanding. The 16th is perhaps the trickiest hole on the course, with a dogleg right and usually a long second shot into a small green. Take an iron off the tee and hit the middle of the fairway.

9 Canyamel

Canyamel Golf Club, Urb.Canyamel Golf Canyamel Avda. D'Es Cap Vermell, 07580 Mallorca
TEL: 971 84 13 13 **FAX:** 971 84 13 14
WWW: golfcanyamel.com
EMAIL: casaclub@golfcanyamel.com
LOCATION: *60km from Palma through Manacor and on towards the town of Arta. Signposts for Canyamel Golf exist at the other side of Arta.*
COURSE: *18 holes, 5841m/6388yd, par 73, SSS 71*
GREEN FEES: ££££+
FACILITIES: *Clubhouse, driving range, buggy hire, hand trolley hire, putting green, practice bunker, golf tuition, club repair, club hire, balls for hire, pro-shop, restaurant, bar and snacks, changing rooms and showers.*
VISITORS: *A handicap certificate is required during the winter months.*

Architect Pepe Gancedo makes great use of the varied landscape on this course to create a venue with plenty of character and challenge. He has also brought into play some interesting man-made antiquities.

The 5th is a spectacular par 3. Too much ambition will result in the ball falling off the steep embankment to the rear. The outstanding hole of the course for good players is the par 4 9th. An ancient stone hut stands in the middle of the fairway at around 182m/200yd off the tee. A precise drive will clear this and leave an excellent attacking position to the elevated green 137m/150yd on.

The back nine has tricky greens. The 13th is a tight drive and you need to hit it clean to set up for a shot at the green. It is possible to reach the green safely by playing to the right.

Above: The 5th green at Canyamel is perched on the side of a hill.

10 *Pula*

Pula Golf Club, Ctra. Son Servera–Capdepera 07550 Mallorca
TEL: *971 81 70 34* **FAX:** *971 81 70 35*
LOCATION: *Through Arta turn right for Canyamel and follow signposts on the road from Son Servera to Capdepera.*
COURSE: *18 holes, 6003m/6565yd, par 71, SSS 71*
GREEN FEES: *££££*
FACILITIES: *Clubhouse, driving range, buggy hire, hand trolley hire, pitching and putting greens, practice bunker, golf tuition, club repair, club hire, pro-shop, restaurant, bar and snacks, changing rooms and showers.*

Pula has built up a reputation partly because of the celebrity tournament that it holds each year with Claudia Schiffer and others, such as Bernhard Langer, taking part. The clubhouse and even the toilets are decorated with pictures of the stars and dignitaries that take part in the competition. The pro-shop staff will also regale you with tales of the rich and famous. However, the course is decidedly average, playing over rolling terrain with occasional views of the Mediterranean. The fees are also rather expensive for what is on offer.

The 1st is a lengthy par 4 to a small green for openers. The 2nd crosses a wide *barranca* but is an easy par 3. The interesting holes begin at the 5th, a par 3 with water right. The 7th is a nice dogleg right with ponds along the right while the 8th is a huge par 5 with a difficult second shot to clear the long pond. The 11th is the most difficult par 3 with bushes to be carried on the right of the green. Hole 18 is an uphill par precariously close to the driving range. The adjacent S'Era de Pula Restaurant is one of the most renowned on the island.

Below: The presence of several ponds helps to tighten Pula's rolling terrain.

11 *Capdepera*

Capdepera Golf Club, Ctra. Arta-Capdepera km3.5, 07570 Arta, Mallorca
TEL: *971 81 85 00* **FAX:** *971 81 81 93*
WWW: *golf@capdeperagolf.com*
EMAIL: *capdeperagolf@ctv.es*
LOCATION: *Palma to Manacor and Arta then on towards Cala Ratjada. Capdepera Golf is on the left between Arta and Cala Ratjada.*
COURSE: *18 holes, 6273m/6860yd, par 73, SSS 72*
GREEN FEES: *££££*
FACILITIES: *Clubhouse, driving range, buggy hire, hand trolley hire, putting green, practice bunker, golf tuition, club repair, club hire, balls for hire, pro-shop, restaurant, bar and snacks, changing rooms and showers.*
VISITORS: *During high season (15th Sept–1st June) handicap is required.*

Capdepera Golf is probably one of the best-designed courses on Mallorca.

The first 12 holes play over a relatively flat valley with trees lining most holes and water and bunkers judiciously placed. The 4th hole is the most memorable of a testing group of par 4s. The fairways are slightly narrow and demand considerable drives.

The 13th plays onto the lower slopes of the surrounding mountains, as do the remaining holes. These holes are full of character. Rocks, trees and river gullies all come into play. The 14th is a tough uphill par 4. Some of the tiered tees, such as the 15th, are supported by dry stonework, which adds to this beautiful and exciting layout. The view from the 18th is stupendous.

12 *Pollensa*

Pollensa Golf Club, Ctra. Palma–Pollensa, km49.3, 07460, Mallorca
TEL: *971 53 32 16* **FAX:** *971 53 32 65*
LOCATION: *C713 road Palma-Pollenca, detour to the left before you get to Pollenca.*
COURSE: *9 holes, 5116m/5595yd, par 70, SSS 70*
GREEN FEES: *£££*
FACILITIES: *Clubhouse, driving range, buggy hire, hand and electric trolley hire, pitching and putting greens, practice bunker, golf tuition, club hire, balls for hire, pro-shop and restaurant.*

Jose Gancedo designed this course with a great appreciation for the land he was working with. He seems to have an affinity for terrain that other golf course architects would shy away from and his results are always exciting and scenically excellent. Pollensa, although only nine holes, is no exception. The course is in a peaceful arena, quite sheltered from wind. This is rolling terrain but it is most beautiful both on the course and the views it affords of the surrounding hills and sea. The land is undulating, with olive trees, natural stone walls, two lakes and various tiers. Trees form the main defence and it is sometimes a matter of luck rather than intention if you get off the tee without tangling with one.

This course will be enjoyed by all levels of player, but experienced golfers in particular will appreciate Gancedo's design.

Above: Capdepera offers an excellent design and a stirring challenge.

REGIONAL DIRECTORY

Where to Stay

The five-star **Gran Hotel Son Net** above the village of Puigpunyent a few kilometres north of Palma (971 14 70 00) is probably the best 'boutique' hotel on the island. The service is supreme and the experience is of absolute elegance. Some might find it a little overbearing, but a few hours by their ultra-classy pool and all will be forgiven. More closely situated to town is the five-star **Grand Luxe Son Vida** (971 79 00 00) with access to its two courses, Son Vida and Son Muntaner. Ask for a Superior Room with views across Palma – it is well worth the extra as the standard rooms are in need of upgrading. It is worth staying here or at its sister **Arabella Parc**, (971 79 99 99), which is newer but without the views, in order to play on Son Muntaner.

Much less costly and possibly better situated for golf on the west side of Mallorca is **Marina Portals Nous** (971 67 75 00). This is not quite a package-holiday palace, and has a good mix of European guests, but the rooms are excellent and the price, including dinner, is just right. You will also be in the right place to stroll the five minutes to the port for some supreme restaurants. To the east of Palma the place to stay is the **Marriott Son Antem Golf Resort and Spa** (0800 221222). This has two courses, a teaching academy and lodgings with American standards of service.

Where to Eat

Mallorcan cuisine could be described as sophisticatedly rustic if that makes any sense. The food is generally hearty and delicious and the more local the better. Fish is always a good bet as are the lamb dishes but be adventurous and try the vegetarian options such as *berenjenas rellenas* (stuffed aubergines – ask the waiter to omit the pork). The best wine is a light white produced in the Binissalem region.

One quality venue is **Restaurante El Pato** (971 75 15 00) in Son Vida Golf clubhouse overlooking the 18th hole. The setting and the food are both classy. The best place on the island for an evening out must be the **Marina Portals** in **Portals Nous** (971 67 75 00), which is even more swish than the upmarket enclave it seems to be modelled on, Marbella's Puerto Banus. A huge variety of yachts squeeze in to this fashionable spot, which is lined with restaurants and boutiques. It is the place to be seen in and to look out for famous faces. The best restaurants are **Bistro Del Tristran** (971 67 61 41), a grandiose place with waiters and waitresses decked out in cream tails. The food is also lavish both in presentation and content, if a little unrelenting in its fussiness. **Esdi's** (971 67 69 81) along the quay

Below: Like Marbella's Puerto Banus, Mallorca's Portals Nous is the place to see and be seen.

is more relaxed, as is **Flanigan's** (971 67 61 17), but there are a dozen good eateries of every description to choose from and tables are usually available.

To the east of the island next door to Pula Golf is **S'era de Pula** (971 56 79 40). This restaurant has an international reputation. Another of the island's best restaurants is **El Olivo** (971 63 90 11), with charming decor and views of the mountains. They serve nouvelle cuisine with various Mallorcan/Mediterranean influences.

Where to Go
Apart from the view from the Son Vida hotel, the best views of Palma are from the historic **Castello de Bellver**. You cannot fail to notice the great **Gothic Cathedral** rising above the yachts by the old harbour. Most tourists are directed to the caves interspersed along the east coast when they are looking for distraction. The **Cuevas del Drach (Dragon's Caves)** and the **Cuevas de Arta** are the most awe-inspiring.

An evening on the port at **Portals Nous** is good for the constitution; wear your dark glasses and pretend to be rich and famous – everyone else does. The port is a more modern version of Marbella's Puerto Banus, but the yachting crowd seem to be gradually converting to Mallorca. There is a railway north of Palma to Puerto Pollensa that is most popular. The inland road to **Puerto**

Above: Besides hundreds of opulent yachts, Portals Nous has some of Mallorca's best restaurants.

Pollensa offers a scenic drive and the unspoilt resort is well worth a day or two's stay as it is quiet and lovely. Island hopping is an alternative but not likely if you are here to play golf. **Menorca** is slower and less commercial while **Ibiza** might be a tad too lively. There is no airport on the smallest of the Balearic Islands, **Formentera**, which is just south of Ibiza – a hydrofoil takes around a bumpy half an hour. Now that the hippies have left there is little to do there but hang out on the nudist beaches.

Useful numbers
Fomento del Turismo de Mallorca
Constitucio 1
1 Palma 07001
Tel: 971 72 53 96
Fax: 971 71 35 40
www.caib.es

Federation of Balearic Golf
Av. Jaume III, 17-1 Despacho 16
Palma de Mallorca
Tel: 971 72 27 53
Fax: 971 71 17 16

Chapter 7

The Canary Islands

The Canary Islands lie more than 1000km (620 miles) to the south of mainland Spain, and just 110km (60 miles) off of North Africa's Atlantic coast. There are seven islands in all, with half a dozen small islets created 14 million years ago by erupting volcanoes. As staging posts for trans-Atlantic sailing voyages and the age-old trade routes down the West coast of Africa, each of the main islands has developed its main towns around its ports.

The tourism infrastructure on the three main islands of Gran Canaria, Tenerife and Lanzarote is very well advanced. In fact, as a destination for golf and tourism, the Canaries could not be better. In the winter the temperatures rarely dip below 19°C and through the summer,

with cooling sea breezes, rarely top 25°C. June and July can be good golfing months here with temperatures of around 25°C and the fairways almost empty. August through October sees hotter spells, but near the coast it is still quite tolerable.

Getting to the Canaries is relatively easy with frequent charter flights leaving regularly from most British and European airports. Prices for flight-only or package deals are reasonable in the summer but rise dramatically in the winter. It is worth investigating prices for do-it-yourself, flight-only packages and allowing the hotel to book your golf as opposed to complete golf packages. The greatest advantage is in the standard of hotel that you can book.

The Canary Islands draw many visitors, particularly in the winter when sunshine is almost guaranteed. Germany tops the tourist numbers, with Sweden and the UK close

Left: Los Gigantes is a quieter alternative on the south coast of Tenerife. Above: Amarilla Golf Club, Tenerife.

behind. There are times through the winter when it can be difficult to find accommodation.

Tenerife

Tenerife is the largest of the islands and the one that attracts the most visitors. The triangular-shaped land mass is dominated by Spain's highest peak, Mount Teide, an extinct volcano which imposes itself, usually covered with snow, on every inland view. It is certainly impressive from the air and more so if you travel inland to view it closer. The mountain causes two distinct climatic zones on the island, with the north being lush and often cloudy and the south sun-baked and arid. Be aware if you travel to see Mount Teide that it is much cooler on the mountain, and warm clothing will be needed.

In the past Tenerife has had limited appeal to golfers with only one serious course in the south and Real Golf de Tenerife, a private club that admits visitors on a limited basis, in the north. Compared with mainland Spain the destination was more for winter sunbathers who enjoyed the occasional fun round. Now there are six courses, with high

standards being set by the newcomers. It seems that the Canary Island authorities have woken up to the possibilities of golf and its high-spending devotees.

For alternative entertainment to golf, Tenerife offers a vibrant nightlife in the busy resorts of Playa de Las Américas and Los Cristianos. Other towns on the south such as Los Gigantes or the Costa Adeje are quieter. To the north, Santa Cruz and Puerto de la Cruz are both interesting, but with the new courses developing on the south coast perhaps not so likely to be on an itinerary for golfers.

Gran Canaria

On the same latitude as Florida, it seems that Gran Canaria has also only just

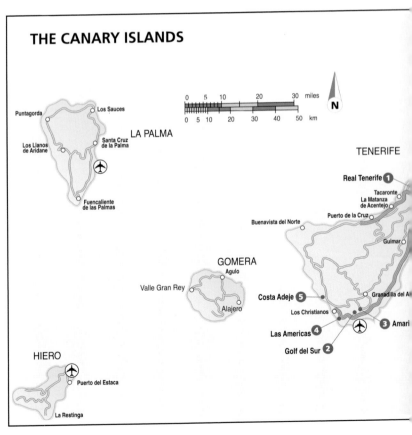

THE CANARY ISLANDS

woken up to the potential that it holds as a golf destination. The recently-built courses are combined with an increasingly luxurious hotel infrastructure, making the island all the more attractive to the golf fraternity.

The island measures 49km (30 miles) across and is divided into three distinct regions, the mountainous interior, the cosmopolitan city of Las Palmas and its surrounds and the hot arid plains to the south. The island offers a wide variety of scenery and it is worth taking a day off to explore it. If you are particularly adventurous, there are some 320km (200 miles) of trails and footpaths, former links between villages in the mountainous interior. Much of the interior is unspoilt

and protected as a national park or nature reserve. The roads are arduously winding so relax and take a bus trip, available daily from the hotels.

One of Gran Canaria's landmarks is the uninterrupted sand dunes stretching from Maspalomas to Playa del Ingles. These huge Sahara-like dunes cover almost one thousand acres, but the picture postcards belie the fact that they are so near the hotels. Beyond them is the island's famous nudist beach. Playa del Ingles can be quite raucous at night. The more sophisticated hotels and apartments found only one or two blocks away are very acceptable.

Lanzarote is another option for sun and golf but with only one course its appeal is limited. The course is fairly pleasant.

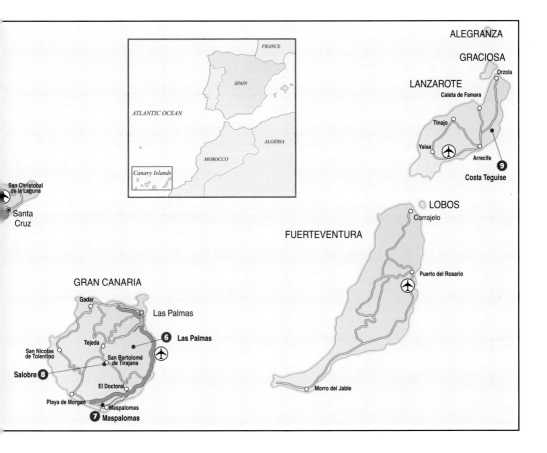

 *Real Tenerife*

*Real Club de Tenerife, Campo de Golf 1,
El Penon - Tacoronte, 38350 La Laguna,
Tenerife*
TEL: *922 63 66 07* **FAX:** *922 63 64 87*
LOCATION: *On the north of the island, 16km
between Santa Cruz and El Puerto de la Cruz
turning off for Guamasa.*
COURSE: *18 holes, 5750m/6288yd, par 71,
SSS 71*
GREEN FEES: *£££*
FACILITIES: *Clubhouse, covered driving range, hand
trolley hire, pitching and putting greens, practice bunker,
club hire, pro-shop, restaurant, bar, changing rooms
and showers.*

*Above: Real Tenerife golf course is traditional and testing,
playing up through fairly dense trees to small, sometimes
sloping greens.*

The north side of Tenerife is generally cooler and more lush. This is most noticeable at Real Club de Teneife. This club, situated in the north of the island, was established in 1932. The course is a green and pleasant tract, although somewhat dated by today's standards and a bit rough in patches.

It is quite an exciting layout to play, however, with trees featuring heavily through a terrain of varying levels. Alternatively, there are several holes that play straight away through long tree-lined avenues. It is interesting to note how verdant this area is compared to the south of the island.

An initial round might prove a little frustrating, but once the up-and-down nature of the course is identified, it can be a lot of fun avoiding the trees, deep gorges and drops and pitching on to the small sloping greens. There is no trickiness to the course as you usually see what you are getting. The challenge lies in getting there both in strokes and, in some instances, walking as some holes are noticeably steep.

The clubhouse is cool and relaxing and the views of Mount Teide from the course are spectacular.

Golf del Sur

Golf del Sur, Urb. Golf del Sur, 38660 San Miguel de Abona, Tenerife
TEL: *922 73 81 70* **FAX:** *922 78 52 72*
WWW: *www.canaryweb.es/golfsur*
EMAIL: *golfsur@canaryweb.com*
LOCATION: *Exit 24 off motorway towards Los Abrigos and entrance is well marked.*
COURSE: *18 holes, 5543m/6062yd, par 72, SSS 72*
GREEN FEES: *££££*
FACILITIES: *Clubhouse, driving range, buggy hire, hand trolley hire, pitching and putting greens, practice bunker, golf tuition, club repair, club hire, pro-shop, restaurant, bar and showers.*

This has been Tenerife's main golf facility for several years, although the younger contenders are now usurping it. Designed by Pepe Gancedo and opened in 1987, the course has hosted a number of international events and good players enjoy the pinpoint accuracy required to avoid trouble. Its 27 holes are quite challenging, but there are certain idiosyncrasies that golfers will either find endearing or frustrating. The North and South combination is the most demanding while the 'links' nine-hole section is ideal for less experienced players. The fairways and greens are silky smooth, but the rough is rocky or downright dangerous. As for the bunkers, they are filled with black volcanic gravel that are a touch too coarse for most players' precious wedges.

Although the fairways are wide with no dividing rough (apart from a few palms and bushes), the large, well-positioned bunkers and occasional water hazard or deep cactus-encrusted gorges demand accurate placement. The 4th is probably the best example; a gradual climbing fairway is flanked by a cavernous gorge on the right side of this right dogleg and a series of gaping black bunkers squeeze in from the left. There are lovely views from this hole across the course to the serene Atlantic waters.

Below: Black volcanic bunkers are Golf del Sur's trademark. The North and South nine-hole courses are a good combination, while the 'links' section is more suited for higher handicaps.

3 *Amarilla*

Amarilla Golf and Country Club, Urb. Amarilla Golf,
38630 Las Galletas, Tenerife
TEL: *922 73 03 19* **FAX:** *922 78 55 57*
EMAIL: *amarilla@redkbs.com*
LOCATION: *Take exit 24 off the motorway towards*
Las Galletas.
COURSE: *18 holes, 6077m/6645yd, par 72, SSS 70*
GREEN FEES: *£££*
FACILITIES: *Clubhouse, driving range, hand trolley*
hire, pitching and putting greens, practice bunker, club
hire, pro-shop, restaurant, bar, swimming pool and
showers.

Donald Steel designed this course set close to the seaside cliffs on the south of the island. The location is excellent but the course is generally mediocre. However, more money is being spent on greenkeeping while some of the holes have seen major refurbishment – so things can only improve. The most memorable holes are by the water, such as the par 3 5th or the similar 12th. These holes face one another in opposite directions so any influence of the wind will generally be reversed. Otherwise, there is plenty of room on the wide fairways with little trouble unless you hook or slice.

The course is set on the landing path for Tenerife's main airport, but there is relatively little noise from the aeroplanes as they glide in towards the runway.

4 *Las Américas*

Golf Las Américas, 38650 Playa de las Américas
Tenerife
TEL: *922 75 20 05* **FAX:** *922 79 52 50*
LOCATION: *Motorway exit 28.*
COURSE: *18 holes, 6039m/6604yd, par 72 ,*
SSS 72
GREEN FEES: *£££*
FACILITIES: *Clubhouse, driving range, hand trolley*
hire, pitching and putting greens, golf tuition, club hire,
pro-shop, restaurant, bar and showers.

Golf Las Américas was opened in 1997. Its 18 holes are set in a natural amphitheatre overlooked by craggy slopes with wide sweeping views of the sea on the course's higher aspects. From the visitors' tees it is not a daunting length. The terrain is relatively flat, with some slopes. It is often crossed by deep ravines caused by ancient streams making their way from the steep mountains to the sea.

There is much water in evidence and these man-made lakes come into play on eight occasions. The 13th is a par 3, encircled by water with two ponds ahead of the green with another to the right and a larger lake to the left. The putting surfaces are generally large and fast, especially with the warm breezes blowing over from the sea. While the course is still evidently new with rather sparse plantings of small pine and more mature palm trees, its fine condition is a credit to the work of the greenkeepers.

Above: Golf Las Américas opened in 1997 and has magnificent views from the clubhouse.

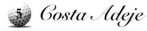

Costa Adeje

Costa Adeje Golf Club, Apdo. De Correos No.3,
38670 Adeje, Tenerife
TEL: *922 71 0000* **FAX:** *922 71 04 84*
LOCATION: *Towards Guia de Isora on the TF. C822 turn left towards La Caleta.*
COURSE: *27 holes, 6280m/6868yd, par 72, SSS 72*
GREEN FEES: *££££*
FACILITIES: *Clubhouse, driving range, hand trolley hire, pitching and putting greens, golf tuition, club hire, pro-shop, restaurant, bar and showers.*

With the opening of several new courses planned on the islands of Tenerife and Gran Canaria, quality courses are now emerging. At Costa Adeje, the renowned maestro of Spanish golf architecture, Pepe Gancedo, has injected modern features such as mounding around the greens. However, he has generally made the course fit the land and the features that were already present.

Below: Costa Adeje fits well into the surrounding natural terrain.

There are 27 holes on offer, with ancillary practice areas and a splendid new clubhouse. There are views to the island of La Gomera across the shimmering Atlantic water, along with aspects of Playa de las Américas and the Adeje mountains. More than 5000m/5470yd of stone wall terracing, former banana plantations, has been restored and forms an integral part of the course.

The main course kicks off with a long par 5. This features strategic bunkering but is fairly straightforward. The par 3s, such as the 2nd, incorporate tiered greens to add to their challenge but again these are manageable. The course then turns towards the water and becomes surprisingly testing for the rest of the round. There are many 'risk and reward' situations where the better golfer can go for birdie opportunities, but bunkering and water will make the more careful club golfer settle for possible par. Another aspect is the banking around and coming into the greens that can kick a well-struck approach into trouble.

6 Las Palmas

Real Club del Las Palmas, Bandama, 35380 Santa Brigida, Gran Canaria
TEL: *928 35 10 50* **FAX:** *928 35 01 10*
EMAIL: *rcglp@step.es*
LOCATION: *Situated in Bandama. 14 km west and inland from Las Palmas.*
COURSE: *18 holes, 5915m/6469yd, par 71, SSS 70*
GREEN FEES: *£££*
FACILITIES: *Clubhouse, driving range, hand trolley hire, pitching and putting greens, practice bunker, golf tuition, club hire, caddy, pro-shop, restaurant, bar, swimming pool, tennis court, horse riding and showers.*
VISITORS: *This is a private members club that allows green fee payers weekday mornings only and a handicap certificate is essential.*

This course was established by English traders in 1891 and is the oldest golfing society outside the UK. The course had to be moved from the rapidly developing urban sprawl of Las Palmas into the mountains and Mackenzie Ross helped with the construction. The course is perched on the side of a long-extinct volcanic rim, with spectacular views of the mountains, city and sea.

The course is a series of banked fairways spread over a gradual decline neatly defined by palms, pines and mimosa bushes. It can be a challenge. The choice of club off the tee is important. The greens are well bunkered and often raised above the fairway, so good pitching skills are needed to attack the pin. The food in the clubhouse is quite exceptional.

Right: The 'terraced' fairways of Las Palmas on Gran Canaria.

7 Maspalomas

Golf Maspalomas, Junto a la Playa de Maspalomas, 35100 Gran Canaria
TEL: *928 76 25 81* **FAX:** *928 76 82 45*
LOCATION: *South motorway, towards Maspalomas.*
COURSE: *18 holes, 6417m/7017yd, par 73, SSS 73*
GREEN FEES: *££££*
FACILITIES: *Covered driving range, buggy hire, hand trolley hire, pitching and putting greens, practice bunker, club repair, club hire, pro-shop, restaurant, bar and showers.*

Maspalomas is more of a holiday course, which over the past few years has proved exceptionally popular with Swedish and German visitors, especially through the winter months. It used to be essential to book tee times months in advance, although this situation might have changed with the opening of Gran Canaria's three new courses.

The course is flat and uninspiring with little rough. It is ideal, perhaps, for inexperienced golfers and long enough for big drivers to get some thrills. Mackenzie Ross provided good approach areas with well-bunkered greens. This adds a touch of exhilaration, but generally the course is somewhat outdated. A wind coming off the nearby water occasionally adds some spice.

Salobre

*Salobre Golf Club and Resort, Urb. El Salobre km.53
San Bartolome de Tirajana, Las Palmas, Gran Canaria*
TEL: *928 06 18 28* **FAX:** *928 06 18 29*
EMAIL: *salobregolf@satocan.com*
LOCATION: *Exit for Salobre Golf at km53, off the
GC1 motorway ten minutes' drive between Maspalomas
and Puerto Rico.*
COURSE: *18 holes, 6145m/6720yd, par 71, SSS 69*
GREEN FEES: *£££*
FACILITIES: *Clubhouse, driving range, hand and electric
trolley hire, pitching and putting greens, practice bunker,
golf tuition, club hire, pro-shop, restaurant, bar and
showers.*
VISITORS: *Handicap required – 30 for men and 36 for
women.*

Set in the hills behind Maspalomas and overlooking the sea, the first 18 holes of this new American-style resort were completed in late 2000. Three hotels are nearing completion and a second 18-hole course will open in 2002. Salobre is set to become one of the main attractions on Gran Canaria. The existing course is divided into four holes of par 5, nine holes of par 4 and five holes of par 3. The designer, Roland Favrat, has blended the golf course into the topography, using indigenous vegetation such as gigantic cacti, yuccas and Canary palms.

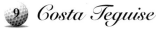

Costa Teguise

*Costa Teguise Golf Club, Urb. Costa Teguise, 35080
Arrecife, Lanzarote*
TEL: *928 59 05 12* **FAX:** *928 59 04 90*
LOCATION: *Towards la Fundación Cesar Manrique on
the Costa Teguise road.*
COURSE: *18 holes, 5842m/6389yd, par 72,
SSS 72*
GREEN FEES: *£££*
FACILITIES: *Clubhouse, driving range, hand and electric
trolley hire, pitching and putting greens, practice bunker,
golf tuition, club hire, pro-shop, restaurant, bar and
showers.*

Lanzarote is a remarkable landscape with its volcanic crags and black beaches. But more remarkable are the lush fairways and greens of Costa Teguise Golf Club in the middle of the island. Surrounded by palm trees and cacti along with banks of dazzling flower beds it is an oasis in this rather stark background.

The fairways tend to be long and comfortably wide with small circular greens that can be run on to. Players who can employ the links-style of bump-and-run into the greens could do well here. Black volcanic sand fills the bunkers, but these are not overly penal and quite easily avoided. The course is only mildly rolling and therefore is easy to walk.

*Left: Salobre Golf Club and
Resort is one of the Canary
Islands' newest golf
developments, and is sure to
attract golfers from all over
Europe and beyond.*

REGIONAL DIRECTORY

Where to stay

Tenerife

There are thousands of hotel rooms in the south of Tenerife and all are within a short drive of the five golf facilities. Most of the better hotels will offer golf packages with reduced green fees, so telephone in advance and ask for their details. The **Hotel Jardín Tropical** (922 74 60 00) is one of the best hotels on Tenerife. It is an island of repose set near the busy beach prominade of Playa de las Américas. Step outside though and it's bedlam. If you don't want to look at timeshares buy a German newspaper and display it prominently. The five-star **Hotel Reina Isabel** (928 26 01 00) is situated directly on the Las Canteras Beach with its own hammocks and sunshades. The new hotels on the Costa Adeje are supreme and if you want to go all the way, the five-star luxury **Gran Hotel Bahia del Duque** (922 74 69 00) is an excellent choice.

Gran Canaria

There are some ritzy hotels around Maspalomas that are well suited to the golfing mentality. The **Hotel Maspalomas Princess** (928 14 31 57) is in the thick of the action near the Maspalomas Dunes with the Maspalomas Golf Club only a five-minute taxi ride away. The five-star **Steigenberger La Canaria** (928 15 04 00) is ultra-luxurious with all the in-house amenities you would need. Close to Real Golf Las Palmas on the west side of the island is the **Hotel Golf Bandama** (928 35 33 54), with views over the pool to the golf course. This cosy hotel, which has 27 double rooms with terraces and a heated swimming pool, is surrounded by a colourful tropical garden.

Where to Eat

Tenerife

The Meson La Cuadra in Las Palmas (928 24 33 80) is an excellent tapas bar with an adjoining restaurant that specialises in locally grown produce. For a meal with a view, the upper floor of 'La Parrilla' restaurant of the **Hotel Reina Isabel** (928 26 01 00) offers one of the island's best à la carte restaurants. It also has an excellent wine cellar. **Hotel Jardín Tropical** (922 74 60 00) has five restaurants to choose from. **El Patio** in the village of Adeje (922 75 01 00) must be reserved for a special night out and should definitely be on the itinerary.

Gran Canaria

Most of the better hotels offer half-board and the

Below: The spectacular drive up to Mount Teide on Tenerife.

buffet meals are usually excellent. If you are out and about a good rule is to eat where the Germans do, as the standards that they demand are always high. **The Orangerie** in Maspalomas (928 14 08 06) is an upmarket outing which may be welcomed, as quality food can be a rarity among the mass-tourism eateries.

Where to go

Tenerife offers shopping and museums in its capital of **Santa Cruz,** but be prepared for crazy parking – vehicle abandonment would be a more appropriate term – and raised blood pressure. Use public transport into the city. A ferry service has recently opened up the island of **La Gomera**. Columbus set sail from La Gomera and two months later discovered America. Things have only changed marginally on the island since then and compared to the other developed islands, La Gomera is very quiet.

Gran Canaria

Gran Canaria's **mountainous interior,** which rises to around 1950m, is best explored by bus; there are organised pick-ups from every major hotel. **Deep-sea fishing** for Blue Marlin, shark, barracuda and smaller fish is available out of **Puerto de Mogán**. Otherwise these holiday hot spots are designed to part tourists from their money. Evenings are meant for eating and drinking in the hundreds of bars and restaurants with little culture in between. Many of the better hotels organise in-house entertainment, often to a surprisingly high standard, and this is open to non-residents.

Tourist Information Centre
Presidential and Tourist Advisory Board
Plaza de los Derechos Humanos
35003 Las Palmas de Gran Canaria
Canary Islands, Spain
Tel: 34 928 36 22 22
Fax: 34 928 36 28 22
E-mail: dpromoc@inecnet.com
www.golf-holidays.com

Below: Las Américas is one of the newer courses, adding to the growing stock of quality golf courses.

Spanish Tourist Offices

SPANISH TOURIST BOARD

C/ José Lázaro Galdiano, n° 6
28071 Madrid
Tel: +34 913 43 35 00
Fax: +34 913 43 34 46

SPANISH TOURIST OFFICES THROUGHOUT THE WORLD

Argentina

Buenos Aires
Oficina Española de Turismo
Florida, 744, 1° P
1005 Buenos Aires
Tel: (54 11 4) 322 7264/326-8213
Fax: (54 11 4) 322 5923
Email: buenosaires@tourspain.es
For Argentina, Bolivia, Chile, Ecuador, Paraguay, Peru and Uruguay.

Austria

Vienna
Spanisches Fremdenverkehrsamt Wien
Walfischgasse, 8/14
A-1010 Wien
Tel: (43 1) 512 95 80
Fax: (43 1) 512 95 81
Email: viena@tourspain.es
For Austria, Czech Republic, Hungary, Slovakia and Slovenia.

Belgium

Brussels
Office Espagnol du Tourisme
Avenue des Arts, 21
1000 Bruxelles
Tel: (32 2) 280 19 26/(32 2) 280 19 29
Fax: (32 2) 230 21 47
Email: bruselas@tourspain.es
www.tourspain.be
www.tourspain.lu
For Belgium and Luxemburg.

Brazil

Sao Paulo
Escritorio Espanhol de Turismo
Rua Zequinha de Abreu 78, Pacaembu
01250-050 Sao Paulo
Tel: (55 11) 3675 2000, 3675 2001
Fax: (55 11) 3872 0733
Email: saopaulo@tourspain.es
For Brazil.

Canada

Toronto
Tourist Office of Spain
2 Bloor Street West, Suite 3402
Toronto, Ontario M4W 3E2
Tel: (1 416) 961 31 31
Fax: (1 416) 961 19 92
Email: toronto@tourspain.es
www.tourspain.toronto.on.ca
For Canada.

Denmark

Copenhague
Den Spanske Stats Turistbureau
NY Ostergade, 34, 1
1101 Kobenhavn
Tel: (45) 33 15 11 65 (Information)
Fax: (45) 33 15 83 65
Email: spturist@tourspain.es
Email: copenhague@tourspain.es (Official correspondence)
www.spanien-turist.dk
For Denmark, Greenland and Faroe Islands.

Finland

Helsinki
Espanjan Valtion Matkailutoimisto
Mechelininkatu, 12
00100 Helsinki
Tel: (358 9) 441 992
Tel: (358 9) 442 014 (Automatic)
Fax: (358 9) 442 687

Email: helsinki@tourspain.es
For Finland and Estonia.

France

Office Espagnol du Tourisme
43, rue Decamps
75784 Paris Cedex 16
Tel: (33 1) 45 03 82 50
Fax: (33 1) 45 03 82 51
Minitel: 36.15 ESPAGNE
Audiotex: 08 36 68 90 54
Email: paris@tourspain.es
www.espagne.infotourisme.com/plan.htm
For France.

•

Germany

Berlin

Spanisches Fremdenverkehrsamt
Kurfürstendamm, 180
10707 Berlin
Tel: (49 30) 882 65 43 (Information)
Fax: (49 30) 882 66 61
Email: berlin@tourspain.es
For Brandenburg, Saxony-Anhalt, Saxony,
Mecklemburg-Western Pomerania, Turingia,
Poland, Latvia and Lithuania.

Düsseldorf

Spanisches Fremdenverkehrsamt
Grafenberger Allée, 100 (Kutscherhaus)
40237 Düsseldorf
Tel: (49 211) 680 39 80
Fax: (49 211) 680 39 85
Fax: (49 211) 680 39 86
Email: dusseldorf@tourspain.es
For North Rheinland-Westfalia, Palatinate
Rheinland, Saarland.

Frankfurt

Spanisches Fremdenverkehrsamt
Myliusstrasse, 14
60323 Frankfurt/Main
Tel: (49 69) 72 50 33
Tel: (49 69) 72 50 38
Fax: (49 69) 72 53 13
Email: frankfurt@tourspain.es
For Hamburg, Bremen, Hessen, Niedersachen,
Shleswig-Holstein.

Munich

Spanisches Fremdenverkehrsamt
Post Fach N° 151940
80051 München

Schubertstrasse, 10
80336 München
Tel: (49 89) 538 90 75
Fax: (49 89) 532 86 80
Email: munich@tourspain.es
For Bavaria and BadenWürtemberg.

Holland

The Hague (Den Haag)

Spaans Bureau voor Vreemdelingenverkeer
Laan Van Meerdervoort 8A
2517 Aj Den Haag
Tel: (31 70) 346 59 00
Fax: (31 70) 364 98 59
Email: infolahaya@tourspain.es
Email: (for official correspondence)
lahaya@tourspain.es
www.spaansverkeersburo.nl

Italy

Milan

Ufficio Spagnolo del Turismo
Via Broletto, 30
20121 Milano
Tel: (39 02) 72 00 46 17 (Information)
Tel: (39 02) 72 00 43 13 (Automatic)
Fax: (39 02) 72 00 43 18
Email: enteturismospagnolo@interbusiness.it
Email: (for official correspondence)
milan@tourspain.es
For Northern Italy (Piedmont, Trentino-Alto
Adige, Tres Venecias, Veneto, Lombardia, Liguria,
Emilia Romana, Valle de Aosta) and the Republic
of San Marino.

Rome

Ufficio Spagnolo del Turismo
Information Office
Piazza di Spagna, 55
00187 Roma
Tel: (39 06) 678 3106
Direction, Administration and Promotion Office:
Via del Morato, 19
00187 Roma
Fax: (39 06) 679 82 72 .
Email: roma@tourspain.es
For Central and Southern Italy, countries of the
Mediterranean coast (except France), Greece,
Turkey and the Middle East.

Japan

Tokyo

Tourist Office of Spain
Daini Toranomon Denki Bldg., 6F
3 - 1 -10 Toranomon. Minato-Ku
Tokyo 105-0001
Tel: (813) 3432-6141
Fax: (81 3) 3432-6144
Email: tokio@tourspain.es
www.spaintour.com
For Japan, Korea, Taiwan, Hong Kong and China.

Mexico

Mexico

Oficina Española de Turismo
Alejandro Dumas, 211
Colonia Polanco
11560 Mexico DF
Tel: (52 5) 531 17 85, 545 73 22
Fax: (52 5) 255 47 82
Email: mexico@tourspain.es
For Mexico, Costa Rica, Panama, Honduras,
Nicaragua, Guatemala and El Salvador.

Norway

Oslo

Spanske Ambassade Turistavdelingen
Kronprinsensgate, 3
0251 Oslo
Tel: (47) 22 83 40 50
Fax: (47) 22 83 19 22
Email: oslo@tourspain.es
www.tourspain-no.org
For Norway and Iceland.

Portugal

Lisbon

Delegação Oficial do Turismo Espanhol
Av. Sidónio Pais, 28 - 3° Dto.
1050 Lisboa
Tel: (351 1) 354 19 92/354 53 29
Fax: (351 1) 354 03 32
Email: lisboa@tourspain.es
For Portugal.

Russia

Moscow

Tourist Office of Spain
Embassy of Spain
ul. Tverskaya - 16/2
Business Center Galeria aktor, 6th floor
103009 Moscow
Tel: (7 095) 935 83 97
Fax: (7 095) 935 83 96
Email: moscu@tourspain.es
For Russia, Ukrania, Belarus, Uzbekistan and
former USSR states (except for the Baltic states).

Singapore

Singapore

Tourist Office of Spain
Commercial Office of Spain
15, Scotts Road
Thong Teck Building #05-08/09
Singapore 228 218
Tel: (65 7) 32 97 88
Fax: (65 7) 32 97 80
Email: singapore@tourspain.es
(Provisionally located at the Commercial Office of
Spain in Singapore).
For Singapore, Thailand, Malaysia, Indonesia,
Philippines, India, Australia and New Zealand.

Sweden

Stockholm

Spanska Ambassadens Informationsavdelning
Stureplan, 6
11435 Stockholm
Tel: (46 8) 6111992/6114136
Fax: (46 8) 6114407
Email: estocolmo@tourspain.es
For Sweden.

Switzerland

Geneva

Office Espagnol du Tourisme
15, rue Ami-Lévrier, 2° CH-1201 Genève
Tel: (41 22) 731 11 33
Fax: (41 22) 731 13 66
Email: ginebra@tourspain.es
For Ticino, Geneva, Vaud, Fribourg, Neuchatel,
Valais, Jura (French and Italian Switzerland),
and Berne.

Zürich

Spanisches Fremdenverkehrsamt
Seefeldstrasse, 19
CH-8008 Zürich
Tel: (41 1) 252 79 30
Fax: (41 1) 252 62 04
Email: zurich@tourspain.es
For German Switzerland.

United Kingdom

London

Spanish National Tourist Office
22-23 Manchester Square
London W1M 5AP
Tel: (44 207) 486 80 77
Fax: (44 207) 486 80 34
Brochure line: 0891 66 99 20
Email: info.londres@tourspain.es
Email: (for official correspondence)
londres@tourspain.es
www.tourist-offices.org.uk/Spain/index.html
www.uk.tourspain.es
www.tourspain.co.uk
For the UK and Ireland.

United States of America

Chicago

Tourist Office of Spain
Water Tower Place
Suite 915 East
845 North Michigan Avenue
Chicago, IL 60611
Tel: (1 312) 642-1992
Fax: (1 312) 642-9817
Email: oetchi@tourspain.es
Email: (for official correspondence)
chicago@tourspain.es
www.okspain.org
For Illinois, Indiana, Iowa, Kansas, Michigan,
Minnesota, Missouri, Nebraska, North Dakota,
Ohio, Oklohoma, South Dakota, Wisconsin.

Los Angeles

Tourist Office of Spain
San Vicente Plaza Building
Suite 956
8383 Wilshire Blvd.
Beverly Hills, CA 90211
Tel: (1 323) 658 71 88
Fax: (1 323) 658 10 61
Email: oetla@tourspain.es

Email: (for official correspondence)
losangeles@tourspain.es
www.okspain.org
For Alaska, Arizona, California, Colorado, Hawaii,
Idaho, Montana, Nevada, New Mexico, Oregon,
Utah, Washington, Wyoming.

Miami

Tourist Office of Spain
1221 Brickell Avenue
Suite 1850
Miami, FL 33131
Tel: (1 305) 358 19 92
Fax: (1 305) 358 82 23
Email: oetmiami@tourspain.es
Email: (for official correspondence)
miami@tourspain.es
www.okspain.org
For Alabama, Arkansas, Florida, Georgia,
Kentucky, Los Angeles, Mississippi, North
Carolina, Puerto Rico, South Carolina,
TennesseeN, Texas, Bermuda, Colombia,
Caribbean Islands, Venezuela.

New York

Tourist Office of Spain
666 Fifth Avenue
35th Floor
New York, NY 10103
Tel: (1 212) 265 88 22
Fax: (1 212) 265 88 64
Email: oetny@tourspain.es
Email: (for official correspondence)
nuevayork@tourspain.es
www.okspain.org
For Connecticut, Delaware, Maryland,
Massachusetts, Maine, New Hampshire, New
Jersey, New York, Pennsylvania, Rhode Island,
Virginia, Vermont, District of Colombia, West
Virginia.

Index

Author's Acknowledgements

I would like to thank the various regional Spanish tourist offices that lent their assistance. I would also like to thank Tracey and Yvonne for organising the photography and Craig Robertson Snr for helping out with the Tenerife shots. Finally, many thanks to my wife and family for putting up with my absence during the research visits.